AF477848

Diary / Landscape

Diary /

JAMES WELLING

Landscape

WITH AN INTRODUCTION BY **MATTHEW S. WITKOVSKY** / THE UNIVERSITY OF CHICAGO PRESS **CHICAGO + LONDON**

PUBLISHED WITH THE SUPPORT OF
THE COMER FOUNDATION FUND.

The University of Chicago Press, Chicago 60637

The University of Chicago Press, Ltd., London
Photographs © 2015 by James Welling
Introduction © 2015 by Matthew S. Witkovsky
Compilation © 2015 by The University of Chicago
All rights reserved. Published 2015.
Printed in the United States of America

24 23 22 21 20 19 18 17 16 15   1 2 3 4 5

ISBN-13: 978-0-226-20412-3 (cloth)
ISBN-13: 978-0-226-23911-8 (e-book)
DOI: 10.7208/chicago/9780226239118.001.0001

Library of Congress Cataloging-in-Publication Data

Welling, James, photographer.
Diary/Landscape / James Welling ; with an Introduction by
Matthew S. Witkovsky.
        pages   cm
Includes bibliographical references and index.
ISBN 978-0-226-20412-3 (cloth : alkaline paper) —
ISBN 0-226-20412-X (cloth : alkaline paper)—
ISBN 978-0-226-23911-8 (e-book)—ISBN 0-226-23911-X (e-book)
1. Photography, Artistic. 2. Landscape photography. I. Witkovsky,
Matthew S., 1967– writer of introduction. II. Title.
TR654.W4187 2015
779'.36—dc23   2014031914

This paper meets the requirements of ANSI/NISO Z39.48–1992
(Permanence of Paper).

TO DONALD YOUNG

Contents

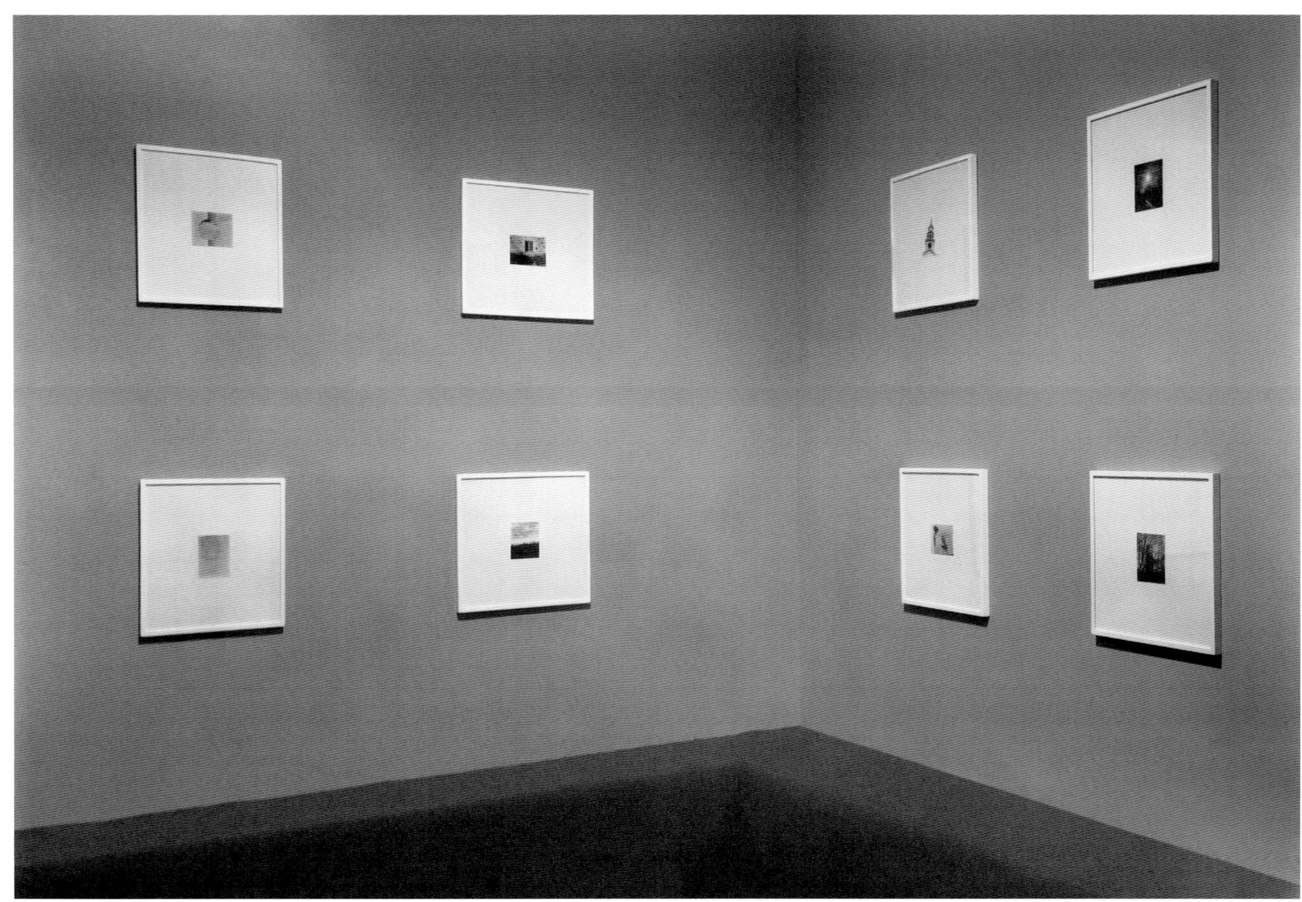

FIGURE 1. *Diary/Landscape*. Installation view, the Kitchen, New York, 1979.

INTRODUCTION

FALSE STARTS
AND FRESH
BEGINNINGS,
OR WELLING'S
WORLD

MATTHEW S.
WITKOVSKY

"As we follow my chronology there are all kinds of false starts and dead ends," James Welling announced in a recent discussion of his earliest years.[1] Welling was referring to his first exhibition outside of art school, an installation in December 1973 that was made up of objects taken from his family house in northern Connecticut. These objects, which Welling had also photographed in his parents' dining room directly before the show, prompted him four years later to create *The Diary of Elizabeth and James Dixon (1840-41) / Connecticut Landscapes, 1977-86*—a series that reimagines false starts, ironically, as the highly productive opposite of dead ends.

Welling, who resided principally in Los Angeles between 1971 and 1978, encountered a three-volume diary during a trip to his parents' new home in Guilford, Connecticut, in the summer of 1977. The diary, written and compiled primarily by Welling's great-great-grandmother, Elizabeth Lord Cogswell Dixon, during her honeymoon tour of Europe in 1840–41,[2] had recently resurfaced among family possessions and appeared in a fresh light to Welling, who on his arrival had begun exploring the southern Connecticut countryside around his parents' new home. The two sets of images—one taken inside, the other out of doors—were thus made in tandem as a private record, initially without the intent to create an art project.

The insight that diary and landscape photographs each informed the other nevertheless pointed to Welling's later practice: his alternation between abstraction and figuration, for example, or between apparently antiquarian series (railroads, buildings by Henry Hobson Richardson, the studio of Andrew Wyeth) and those manifestly engaged with self-reflexive vanguard art, such as the photographs of aluminum foil or gelatin. On returning to Los Angeles in September 1977, Welling considered *Diary/Landscape* (to revert to its short title) a nascent body of work. In January 1979, a first selection of images was shown by Welling's close friend, artist Jack Goldstein, in a two-week group exhibition at the Kitchen in New York (fig. 1).[3] Diary and landscape images would henceforth appear in alternating pairs, selected from over 300 negatives that Welling finally inventoried and finished printing in 1986, out of more than 400 he had made to that date. A definitive set of exhibition prints was never established—diaries, unlike other literary forms, tend not to have an ending. A request from this curator in 2010 led the artist to choose 148 mostly vintage prints, the fullest selection of the series that there will ever be, which now resides with the Art Institute of Chicago.[4]

Most aspects of the undertaking suggest a similarly improvisational approach. For example, Welling did not photograph the pages of the Dixon diary in sequence, and several of the pictures show neither of its volumes but rather one of two additional books made or embellished by Elizabeth Dixon. Other "diary" photographs show heirlooms, while the outdoor shots picture buildings, pets, family, and other scenes that do not fit the genre of landscape. Welling used a variety of photographic papers—including cool Kodak Azo paper, selenium-toned Kodak Studio Proof printing-out paper, and Agfa Portriga Rapid, warmer in tone—along with Polaroid self-developing film and hand-colored prints in isolated instances. Of a piece with this variegated look are disparate echoes of subject matter and printing methods used by contemporary and earlier photographers, from participants in the *New Topographics* exhibition (1975) to members of the Alfred Stieglitz circle, Bauhaus modernists, and various American and European nineteenth-century practitioners. The quality of the prints, judged by conventional photographic notions of balance and mastery, is also highly varied; although many suggest trials or attempts rather than "successes," Welling pointedly included them in his final inventory of the series.

Diary/Landscape thus has an overall shape, but it deliberately lacks the rigorous ordering or assertions of completeness associated with the post-conceptual archive. Welling furthered his project opportunistically on visits home: February and Thanksgiving 1978, Christmas 1979 and January or February 1980, and early 1981 (a very few photographs came later). In this respect, too, it resembled a diary, that is, a collection of short commentary kept only intermittently and mainly at moments of leisure. Many of the photographs were not even printed at the time. Welling turned to these negatives as part of a larger cataloguing effort that he undertook during a one-month residency at Light Works in Syracuse,

New York, in May 1986. The older form of the handwritten diary then merged with the more recent one of the family album: a sequence of pictures that are sometimes printed and assembled only retrospectively. Welling was reviewing in Syracuse all he had done to that date, and for organizational purposes he assigned letters to his various series, with a number for each subsidiary image, ordered roughly chronologically and according to the tonal density of each negative. Tellingly, *Diary/Landscape* was given the first letter of the alphabet; by the mid-1980s, Welling considered it his first fully realized body of photographs.[5]

If the disunified variety of its genres and print types, and its episodic creation, made *Diary/Landscape* out of step with much serious art of the time, so too did its themes of personal and antiquarian history. Welling's longstanding interest in the camera as a mute copying device could seem fitting for a student of his generation, schooled by the first wave of Conceptual artists and familiar with acts of appropriation. He had made artwork with a Xerox machine in 1970 while studying at Carnegie Mellon in Pittsburgh; just four years earlier, Mel Bochner (who had also studied there) had created an entire exhibition from photocopies, a seminal event in the history of American conceptualism.[6] Welling had also presented some magazine advertisements, pure readymades, at his MFA thesis exhibition at California Institute of Arts, in 1974. Yet his study of Elizabeth Dixon's diaries had its beginnings in a teenage fascination with facsimile copies of manuscripts, sparked by seeing one that his great-great-grandfather, James Clarke Welling, had owned and published; the document in question was a letter on emancipation written to Horace Greeley by Abraham Lincoln.[7]

The later discovery that not only James Clarke Welling, but also the Dixons, knew Lincoln and his wife personally (James Dixon had been a congressman and senator from the Polk administration through the Civil War era) gave Welling further motivation to photograph Dixon's journals. It was a mix of personal and national history, in other words, that attracted him initially to the subject of copying. His subsequent education in literary and aesthetic theory, as well as his formidable interest in structural film and Conceptual art, should be seen as diversifying rather than supplanting or completing that youthful attraction. It was in high school as well that Welling received a catalogue on Andrew Wyeth drawings that came illustrated with letters by the artist, again reproduced in facsimile. Welling loves Wyeth's work—he recently created an entire series photographing the American painter's work locations—and he remains unperturbed by the gulf separating this traditional artist from the vanguard concerns of his best friends and teachers at Cal Arts.[8]

Welling's first photographs for the series date to two days after the Fourth of July in 1977, just one year after the United States Bicentennial. Lincoln and the Civil War, colonial New England, a European tour, Independence Day: these quaintly patriotic points of reference fit strangely with the late-1970s art world. They match neither the punk music that Welling and his closest art-school friends made or admired (see *A82* for a lone exception, p. 146), nor the waves of liberation movements swelling and crashing since the sixties; they seem at odds with the hard-headed structuralist and conceptualist works that he had encountered as a student earlier in the 1970s, and equally distant from emerging interests of his own generation, whether these concerned public subjects such as the mass media or the in-your-face intimacy of downtown art scenes. In short, Welling's choice of an inaugural art project might be hastily dismissed as disorganized in its form and conservative in its overtones—a false start or dead end, indeed, with the next two series, *Aluminum Foil* (1980–81) and *Drapes* (1981), arriving to mark a way out of the impasse.

In fact it is not so. *Diary/Landscape* does not escape from public to private histories but rather treats their point of intersection. It manages to be personal and historically minded, yet also expressive of great theoretical awareness and engagement with important issues of the day. It anticipates the series immediately to come but leads elsewhere as well, and for that reason has given Welling much to revisit in recent years. Finally, with its constellation of disparate images and its faint suggestion of curling photographs from a family shoebox, *Diary/Landscape* fits perfectly with much art made since the dawn of the new century, at a moment of general lamentation for the passing of physical snapshots and chemical photography (with all their associated cultural memories). The series is less a cul de sac, ultimately, than an open if meandering road.

Among the very first works in the series are *A95* and *A96*, two landscape pictures printed soon after they were taken (pp. 45 and 52). They evidently show the same scene, a view from the front steps of the Guilford house, from two slightly different vantage points and at different times of day—or with uneven results in printing. To include them both in the inventory, as Welling did in his 1986 review, was already to signal the experimental character of his project. By this is meant not radicalism but testing, and accepting, trial and error. Every work in the series is a study, some more apparently successful than others, and all studies have validity within the framework of an exploratory, diaristic project. Welling did not follow here the legacy of the Bauhaus, with its art-school emphasis on systematic and serial experiments in "basic form," nor did he try common comparative procedures in photography, such as "bracketing," or shifting camera controls up and down one notch to either side of those chosen for the initial exposure. Welling did devour camera manuals by the score in the two years before starting this project. But he deliberately avoided the thoroughness of mid-twentieth-century methods, based on mastery of equipment and materials, in favor of the uncertain but adventuresome efforts of circa 1840—the year of Dixon's diary—when each negative was prepared, exposed, and processed individually, under conditions far more erratic than those found in a modern darkroom. *A95* and *A96*, variant prints made from two separate negatives, are like sketches, quickly drawn and useful as studies. The most common way to approach landscape, for artists or amateurs in the early days of photography, was through sketching, and one could explain both halves of *Diary/Landscape* as a sketchbook (a visual diary) made with a camera.[9]

Welling found his great-great-grandmother's diary volumes later in the week that he took these two pictures. Photographing the diaries crystallized Welling's project as fundamentally concerned with transcription, and with the challenges of investing copy work with subjectivity or historical awareness. In addition to his prodigious reading in technical photographic literature, Welling had been intently studying photographs themselves—but in reproduction. He had bought (and painted from) the Dover Press reissue of Mathew Brady's Civil War photographs in 1975, among other publications where he could see pictures of hilly Pennsylvania or Virginia countryside that looks as terrifyingly lacking in cover as the copse shown in *A95* and *A96*. One way in which public and private histories intersect in *Diary/Landscape* is, indeed, through "period" landscape scenes—photographed in the 1970s, looking like the 1860s—that carry an emotional weight tied simultaneously to the artist's family past and to momentous events in American history: the emancipation of the slaves, Civil War battlefields.

At the same time, Welling made full use of the intellectual remove afforded by working from copies, and he manifestly treated photography as a discipline governed by copying. In a variation on this theme, Welling was intrigued by contemporary photographers who devoted themselves to reproducing lost bodies of work by others. George Tice (born 1938), for example, was featured in a Time-Life book for his work in resurrecting (as platinum prints) the late nineteenth-century lantern slides of Frederick Evans (1853–1943), best remembered then and now as a master platinum printer; and Lee Friedlander (born 1934), who had rediscovered and reprinted a set of turn-of-the-century portraits of prostitutes by New Orleans studio photographer E. J. Bellocq, working, like Tice, from the original negatives (fig. 2).[10] Even masters such as Strand or Eugène Atget were known to Welling principally through reproduction, and in the case of Atget, partly through posthumous prints made by Berenice Abbott (fig. 3). As facsimiles of historical photographs, these modern prints could readily be analogized to the transcriptions of nineteenth-century letters that had earlier fascinated Welling.

This line of interpretation suggests Welling's affinity with the "Pictures Generation" that he helped to found, and there is a good deal of critical literature to support the connection.[11] Welling's copy photography is not, however, a treatise on the simulacrum. *Diary/Landscape* is an homage to photographic modernism—as much a sketchbook of personalities in photography as it is a record of book pages or countryside. The brooding browns and grays of Paul Strand's pictures of the Gaspé Peninsula (fig. 4), or his attention to leaves and tree limbs as emblems of a woodland idyll, can readily be found in Welling's images (*A216, A42, A46* [pp. 91, 49, 63]). Strand's close friend Alfred Stieglitz is summoned as well, in pictures that eternalize a dormer window or gable (*A21, A38* [pp. 144, 124]) or, most especially, in a few views that crest the treetops to show the crisp majesty of a cloud-filled sky (*A30, A85, A161, A178* [pp. 27, 84, 81]). Walker Evans appears, quite straightforwardly, the object of outright borrowing in a couple of absolutely frontal photographs of vernacular pictures and architecture (*A101, A35* [pp. 129, 26]). The fascination of early British and French photographers for fully grown oak or maple trees, symbols of prosperity that graced every gentleman's farmland property, comes through in the numerous tree studies, especially a suite from the series taken in 1979, on a high-school reunion trip to central Connecticut (*A217–A231* [pp. 42, 118, 119, 120]).

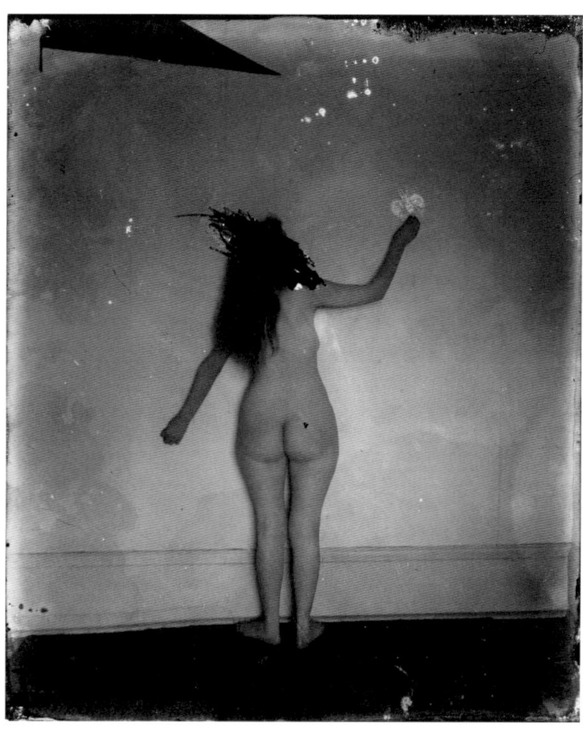

2

3

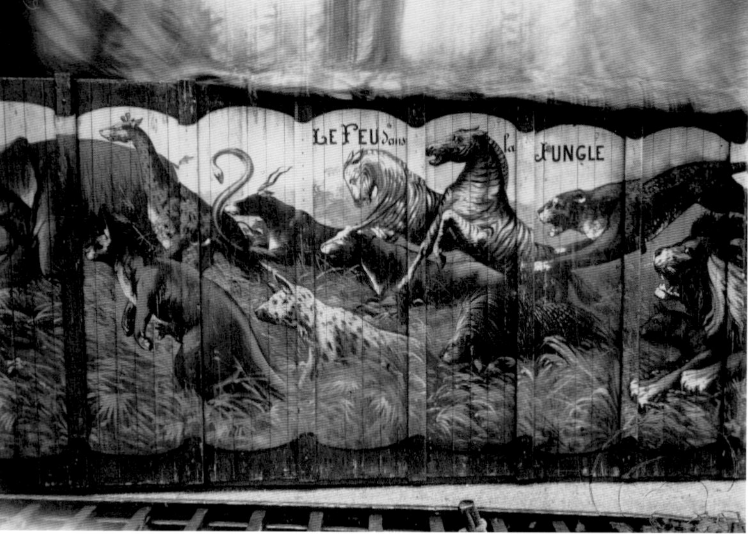

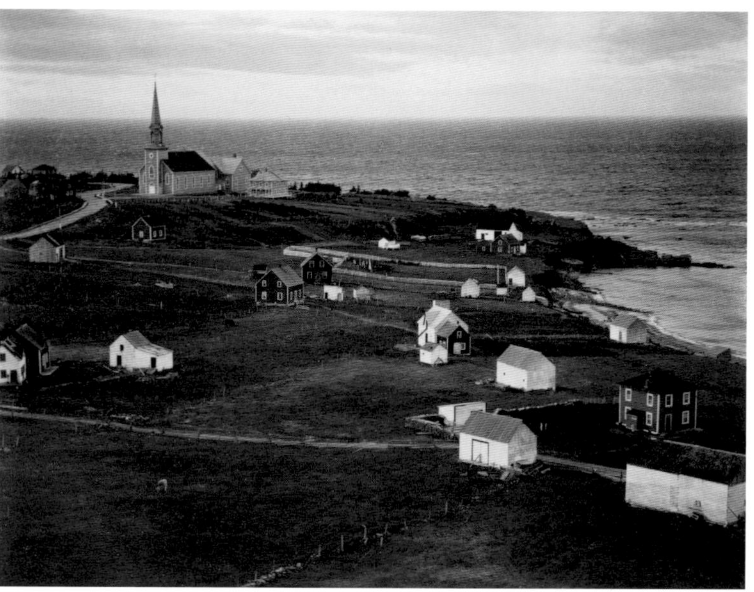

4

FIGURE 2.

E. J. Bellocq (American, 1873–1949), printed by
Lee Friedlander (American, b. 1934). *Storyville
Portrait* (ca. 1912), printed later. Gelatin silver
printing-out paper print. 25.2 × 20.3 cm (image);
25.4 × 20.5 cm (sheet). Restricted gift of Gilda
Buchbinder (2010.511). Photograph: © The Art
Institute of Chicago.

FIGURE 3.

Jean-Eugène-Auguste Atget (French, 1857–1927),
printed by Berenice Abbott (American,
1898–1991). *Fête du Trône* (1926), printed before
1970. Gelatin silver print. 16.8 × 23.1 cm (image/
paper); 33.1 × 25.4 cm (mount). Gift of Robert A.
Taub (2012.256). Photograph: © The Art Institute
of Chicago.

FIGURE 4.

Paul Strand (American, 1890–1976). *Fishing
Village, Gulf of the St. Lawrence, Gaspé* (1929).
Gelatin silver print. 9.2 × 11.7 cm (image/paper).
Art Institute of Chicago, Ada Turnbull Hertle
Fund (1980.69). ©Aperture Foundation Inc., Paul
Strand Archive.

These various names, added to those of Atget or Frederick Evans (still others could be found) give the series the cast of a stylistic compendium. It is as if the diary photographs, which are relatively unified in appearance and recognizably original, contained in their pictured pages commentary on the array of sources referenced in the landscape photographs with which they are interspersed (or interleaved). The commentary is distant yet respectful. These prints may knowingly evoke copy photographs, but the problematics of mechanical reproduction are joined to straightforward admiration and a real interest in predecessors. It is true that the darkroom heroics essential to modernist mastery—vast tonal range, warmth and richness of texture, perfectionist dodging and burning—have been set aside, along with the modernist insistence on absolute clarity and sharp focus. At the same time, Welling's serene compositions emanate a nascent passion for photography.

If the overture to past masters and periods in photography appears bookish, the emotional charge of many pictures makes plain that this artist-scholar is no academic but an autodidact. The picture *A9*, which Welling printed right away and then reprinted numerous times in subsequent years, pointed him specifically toward the marriage of sober theoretical concerns and affective charge (p. 28). *A9* can of course be considered a statement on intertextuality, with "light writing" and handwriting held in productive tension. The handwritten pages, as several commentators have observed, are fragmented and difficult to read, their legibility diminished by lines of writing that show through from the reverse of the paper. The photograph acts not to copy but to cut and layer the manuscript, in the manner of a Derridean *rature*: a crossing out that yet leaves the original word choice visible—and, in French, a close cousin to the word for "failure."[12] Photography here does not write with light so much as it overwrites.

A counterprogrammatic use of the camera lens—a device manufactured to amplify human vision—can readily be found in the landscape pictures too, many of which tend toward the crepuscular and are printed as if veiled in a penumbral gray. Put simplistically, text in the diaries is a bit hard to read, and trees and paths in the landscapes are somewhat hard to see. But the significance of those choices is not exhausted by calling the series a lesson in the deconstruction of meaning. Curator Mark Godfrey, writing recently on Welling's lifelong series *Light Sources*, stated in a general way that Welling courts indecipherability, a condition that Godfrey rightly termed at once frustrating and liberating: "To my mind, the indecipherability of some of Welling's photographs is sometimes associated with failure and brings about (for a viewer) a sense of frustration, irritation, confusion, and deprivation. In other works, however, indecipherability is exhilarating, evocative, emotional, full of possibility: it allows us to experience things in a new and unfamiliar way."[13]

Godfrey's excellent insight can be extended and refined, first by showing that frustration and exhilaration are not complementary but intertwined, and are present in nearly every picture of *Diary/Landscape*. In *A9* as in almost all the diary photographs, Welling has practically caressed the pages, pushing his equipment ever closer to their surface: these sheets of paper are not to be read but cradled.[14] Pages in the diary books were turned and held with gentle pressure for each photograph, often (as in this picture) creating a swell at center that then received a wash of natural sunlight. The writing itself may be hard to decipher in *A9*, but the material characteristics of the ink and the paper sheet are easily apprehended, and sunlight itself has a tangible presence. Welling's attraction to the many pages in Dixon's second diary volume that enclose pressed flowers and leaves further emphasizes materiality even within the flat confines of a book—or a photographic print.

The flowers, for example in *A10* (p. 46), often cover the writing, an arrangement that certainly frustrates legibility; this picture shows the additional *rature* of a strobe glare at the left, which "overwrote" all information on the left side of the negative, as well as excessive selenium toning, which tinted the paper pink in what could be considered another form of deletion through overwriting. These "failures" are nonetheless entirely worth retaining. They mark one entry in the diaristic series—a single set of observations that individuates this print and heightens its emotional appeal. The pressed thistle, blackened in printing, has acquired a sensuous weight against the pink-white page, and the heading "Italy," underlined three times by the diarist, radiates in little ripples its associations of immemorial culture seen on a European tour. Like Elizabeth Dixon's diary entry, the flash exposure and selenium toning were not necessarily to be repeated, nor did Welling wish to test variants to see if he might have greater success. A diary is not a laboratory, though both are spaces for experimentation. But the emotions packed into this small picture—

uncertainty, excitement, apprehension, sensuous discoveries—do continue across the series, as in the pages of their source material, and they push what might otherwise have been a sober copy project into the realm of palpable delights.

The diary books, and a third volume called *Album Wreath* (see for example *A6* [p. 19]), were photographed mostly in the study otherwise used by Welling's father, a room that is pictured just once, in *A257* (p. 126). The scene doesn't fit: its modern furnishings and real-world clutter give a view onto contemporary daily life that explains *a contrario* the pastoral quality essential to this series. The greater age of most structures, such as bridges and houses of fieldstone, or a World War I memorial, accounts only partly for the pastoral effect. Equally important is the steady light, radiant yet dulled even in those pictures taken directly into the sun, as well as a sense of solitude that is conveyed by mostly static compositions. Finally there is the impact of contact printing (from 4 × 5-inch negatives), which Welling undertook, for the earliest works, in a makeshift darkroom that he set up in the basement of the family home. The artist later described this small paper size as necessary to a "facsimile effect," by which he meant that the print would be an exact copy of the negative, and by extension would serve to copy the subject before the lens truly and faithfully. Really, though, what these contact prints convey is a miniature sense of wonder—the magic and elation of a quiet scene coming to light, as described by countless early practitioners of photography working at the time of the Dixons' honeymoon travels.

Only a very few photographs in the series combine diary and landscape views. One shows the diary placed, exceptionally, on the living-room windowsill, lit in summer from the sunstrewn front yard beyond; another, taken in the hard, slanting light of winter, pictures the dining room in full and gives just a hint of the house's back yard (*A295* and *A127* [pp. 92, 33]). The furnishings in *A127* are mostly heirlooms transferred to the care of Welling's parents after the death of his great-aunt, Elizabeth Dixon Welling, whose demise in 1976 had prompted the family move from central Connecticut to Guilford, near the Long Island Sound. Aunt Elsa, as she was called, lived in what Welling remembers as a time warp—born in 1885, she seemed unaccountably to be younger than any of her possessions.

That sense of time travel is fully conveyed in *A127*, which could be an installation view from a New England house museum. For all its apparent pastness, the scene also points to several of Welling's sustained and future interests. Daylight filters through the curtained windows, suffusing the interior and creating an implicit contrast with two tallow candles on the table, as well as the presumably electric candelabra hanging from the ceiling—a study in light sources if ever there was one. Depth compression from Welling's slightly wide-angle lens collapses the room, pointing toward the flatness and abstraction that Welling would spend years exploring. The metaphorical associations attached to curtains and fabric, meanwhile, which must be read into *Drapes*, are plainly dominant in this picture, where white window curtains—particularly those that are drawn at the back of the room—suggest a memorial parlor and the ghosts of past inhabitants. Welling has always claimed a latent high drama for his photographs, and this one seems to carry that narrative potential in broad daylight. "It is [the] dilation and contraction of time," observed art historian David Joselit, "that has consistently marked James Welling's photography."[15]

Speaking recently with fellow artist Sharon Lockhart, Welling commented: "I think that all landscape photographs are a stand-in for abstract art, which is a stand-in for emotion in art. To me it seems very obvious that I'm photographing emotions."[16] Seen so close that they can almost be felt, the diary pages are a quietly emotional landscape, while the landscape views register with equally subdued emotions as a diaristic transcription of "the world on my doorstep."[17]

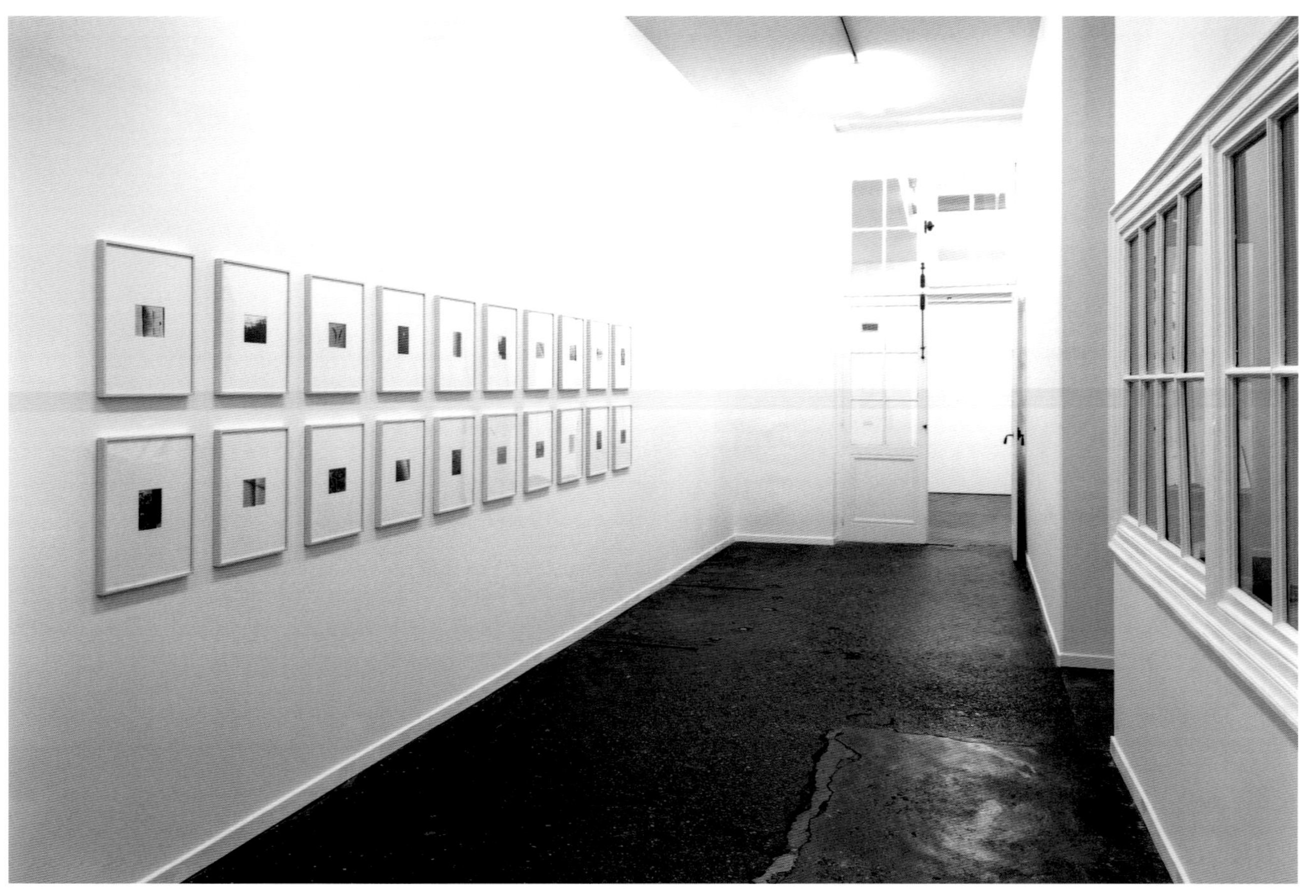

FIGURE 5. *Diary/Landscape*. Installation view, Galerie Nelson, Lyon, France, 1988.

NOTES

1. "The Mind on Fire," James Welling interviewed by Anthony Spira, in *The Mind on Fire* (MK Gallery, Centro Galego de Arte Contemporáneo, and Contemporary Art Gallery of Vancouver, 2014), 127.

2. The diary contains a few entries from 1841 by Elizabeth's husband, James Dixon.

3. *The Mind on Fire*, 160.

4. Group exhibitions involving *Diary/Landscape* after the Kitchen include *Imitation of Life*, Hartford Art School, 1979; and *A Forest of Signs: Art in the Crisis of Representation*, Los Angeles Museum of Contemporary Art, 1989. Solo exhibitions featuring the series begin with Jay Gorney Modern Art, New York, 1988; Galerie Nelson, Lyon, 1989; and the Kunsthalle Bern, 1990, and continue with those at the Wexner Center for the Arts, 2000 (traveled to Baltimore Museum of Art and Los Angeles Museum of Contemporary Art) and the Cincinnati Museum of Art, 2013 (traveled to Hammer Museum, Los Angeles; and Fotomuseum Winterthur). After the show in Bern, which contained 32 prints, Welling did not attempt to assemble a complete set of images of *Diary/Landscape* until approached by the Art Institute.

5. With an increase in retrospective exhibitions and curatorial attention to his earliest work, Welling has expanded the chronology of his first years after art school, such that *Los Angeles Architecture and Portraits* (1976–78), a series shown in a back room at the Kuhlenschmidt/Simon Gallery in 1987, and in 1999 at Leslie Tonkonow Gallery, has entered the canon of finished bodies of work. (The juxtaposition of *Los Angeles Architecture and Portraits* with *Diary/Landscape* in a recent retrospective exhibition, *Monograph* [Cincinnati Art Museum, 2013] made clear the parallel between these two early series, each divided in dialogic halves.) A variety of student projects have deservedly gained attention as well—for example, in the book and exhibition *The Pictures Generation*, organized by Douglas Eklund at the Metropolitan Museum of Art, New York (2009).

6. Bochner, *Working Drawings and Other Visible Things on Paper Not Necessarily Meant to Be Viewed as Art*, School of Visual Arts, December 1966. Published in book form in 1997 by Cabinet des estampes du Musée d'art et d'histoire, Geneva, with Buchhandlung Walther König, Cologne and Picaron Editions, Paris.

7. Welling saw this document in a second-generation reproduction, as published by his relative, see James Clarke Welling, *Addresses, Lectures, and Other Papers* (Cambridge, Mass.: Riverside Press, 1903). The original letter was donated by Elizabeth Dixon's daughter to the Wadsworth Atheneum in 1923.

8. Welling's series *Wyeth* (2010–14) was most appropriately exhibited at the Wadsworth Atheneum, March–July 2012; see Patricia Hickson interview with James Welling, http://www.thewadsworth.org/welling/ (accessed April 2014).

9. Welling had spent four years making watercolors of his parents' earlier property, northwest of Hartford, during the second half of the 1960s; *Mind on Fire*, 150.

10. *Caring for Photographs: Display, Storage, Restoration* (New York: Time-Life Books, 1972); *E. J. Bellocq: Storyville Portraits*, ed. John Szarkowski (New York: Museum of Modern Art with New York Graphic Society, 1970).

11. According to the chronology in *Mind on Fire* (159), Welling met critic and curator Douglas Crimp in the summer of 1977, directly before Crimp opened his foundational exhibition *Pictures*, in September of that year. Welling was already close friends with Jack Goldstein and Troy Brauntuch, two of the four artists in *Pictures*, and he met others in and around the show that summer as well (Robert Longo and Cindy Sherman, for example). Partly in response to Crimp—to indicate what and who was missing from his account at the moment that Crimp published *Pictures* as an article in *October* magazine (Spring 1979)—Welling collaborated with David Salle on an article, "Images That Understand Us" (1980). For more on this article and Welling's place in (and ahead of) the "Pictures Generation," see Eklund (see above, note 5), especially 42–48.

12. Derrida's classic book *Of Grammatology* (1967; Eng. trans. 1976) is appropriate to Welling's project in date of publication as well as content; *Writing and Difference* appeared in 1978. Citing Jacqueline Rose, the art critic Rosalyn Deutsche stressed the need to "hang on to failure" in describing Welling's various works in abstraction; she gave as an example instances where an excess of form-giving light threatens to drown out the image. See R. Deutsche, "Darkness: The Emergence of James Welling," in *James Welling: Abstract* (Brussels and Toronto: Palais des Beaux-Arts and Art Gallery of York University, 2002), 16. Several of the photographs in *Diary/Landscape* bear out this assertion—for example, those in which Welling has pointed his camera at the sun (e.g., *A124* [p. 29]) or tried to shoot a scene with vastly differing light levels in the sky and on the ground (*A161*, *A162* [pp. 84, 82]); or, again, the picture *A96* with which he began the series. All these pictures are "failed" in a conventional sense.

13. Mark Godfrey, "Light, Loss, Love: James Welling's *Light Sources*," in James Crump, ed., *Monograph* (Cincinnati: Cincinnati Art Museum, 2013), 187.

14. To achieve this effect, Welling used a 127mm lens on a Burke and James 4 × 5-inch view camera with its bellows maximally extended.

15. David Joselit, "Surface Histories: The Photography of James Welling," *Art in America* 89, no. 5 (May 2001): 142.

16. "Sharon Lockhart and James Welling in Conversation," in Charlotte Cotton and Alex Klein, eds., *Words without Pictures* (New York and London: Aperture and Thames and Hudson, in collaboration with Los Angeles County Museum of Art, 2010), 460.

17. Catherine Duncan, *Paul Strand: The World on My Doorstep* (New York: Aperture Foundation, 1994).

Diary

OF ELIZABETH AND JAMES DIXON

[1840-41]

CONNECTICUT

Landscapes

[1977-86]

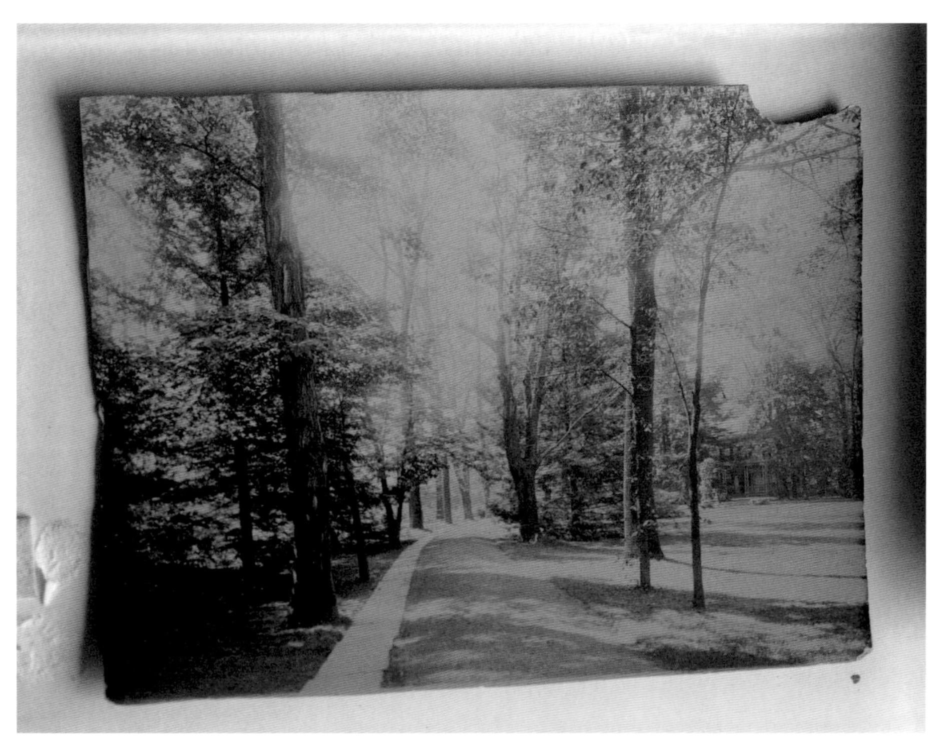

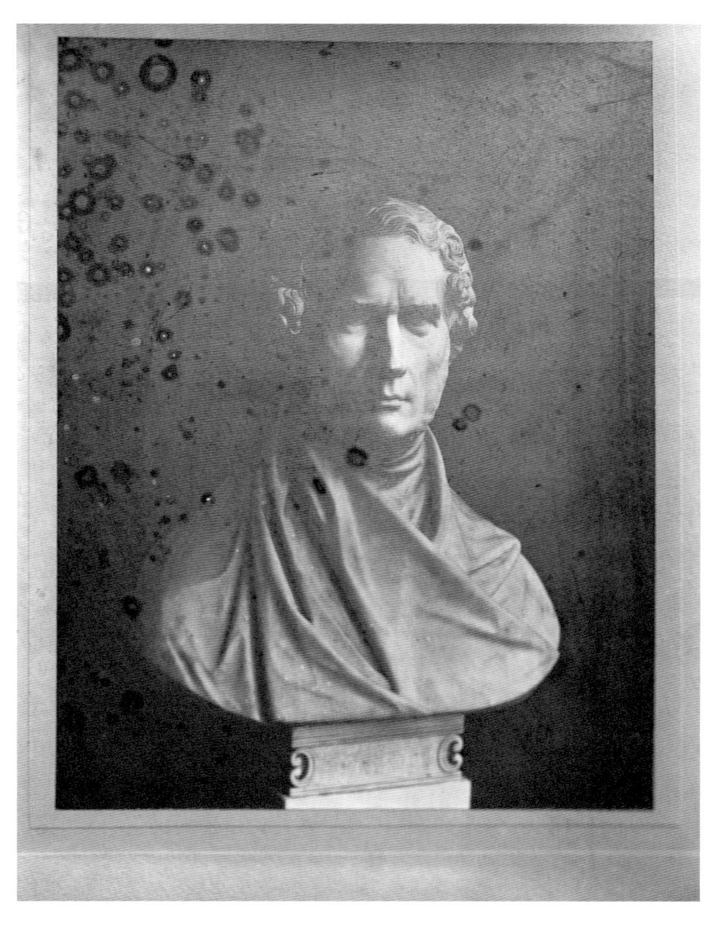

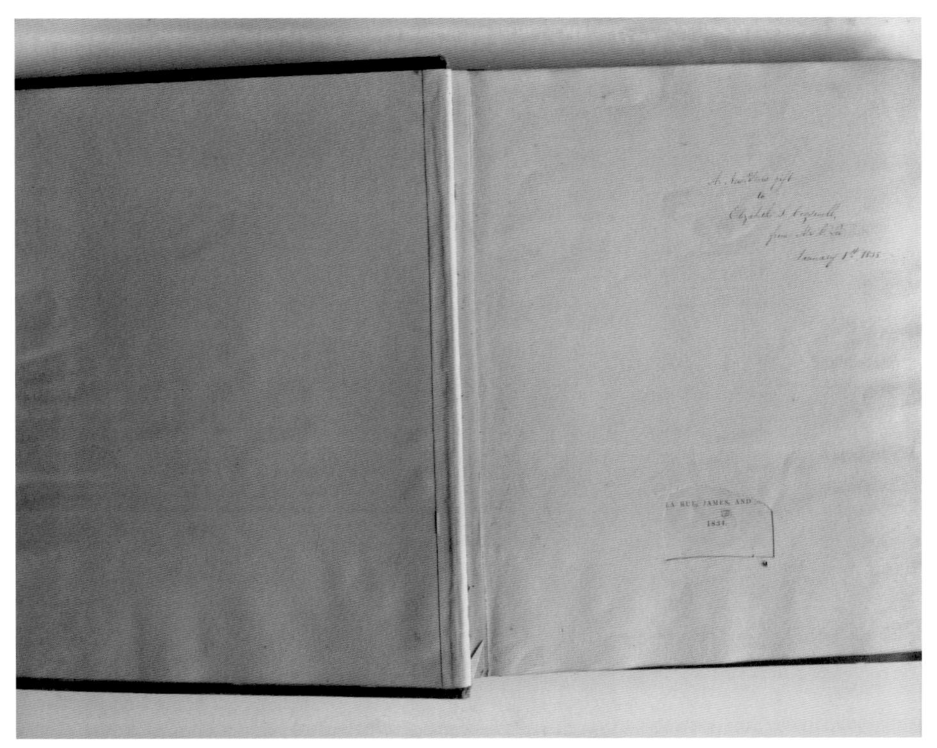

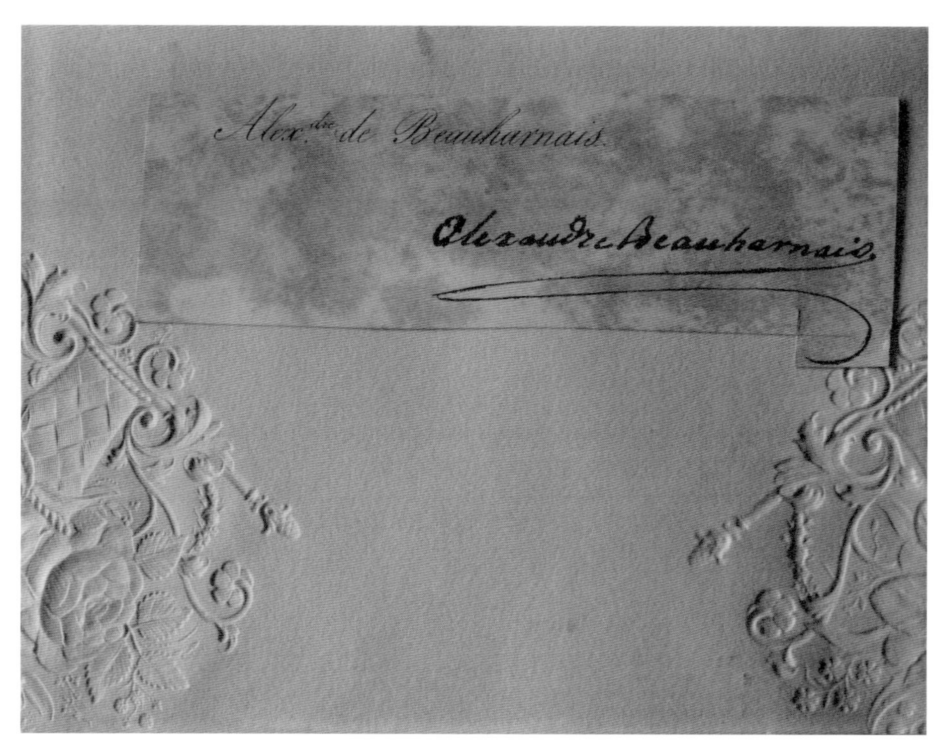
Alex.dre de Beauharnais.
Alexandre Beauharnais.

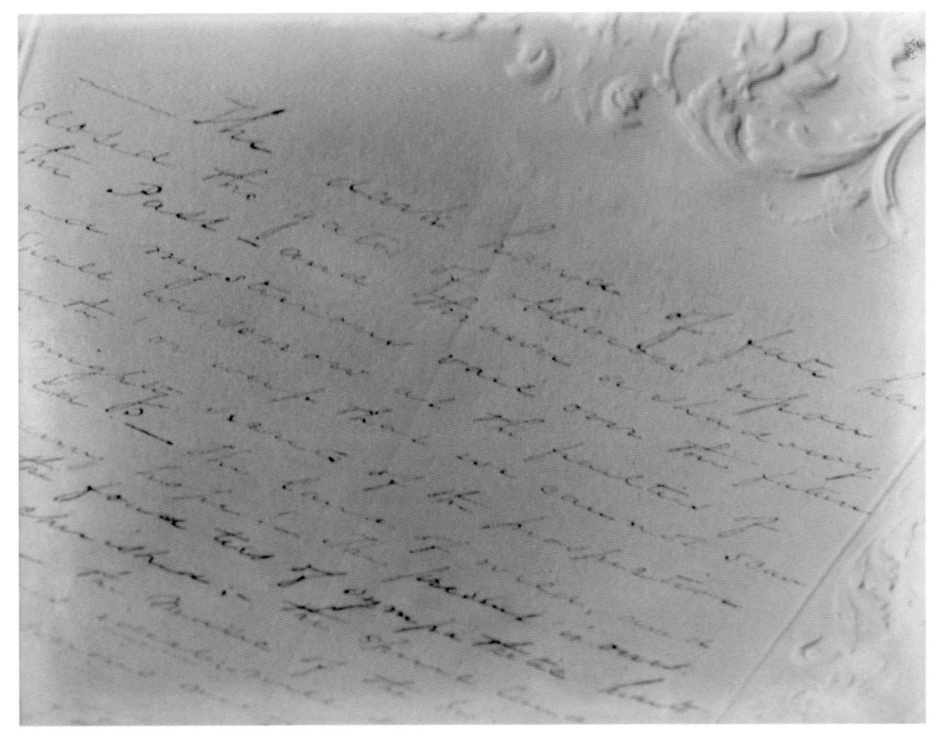

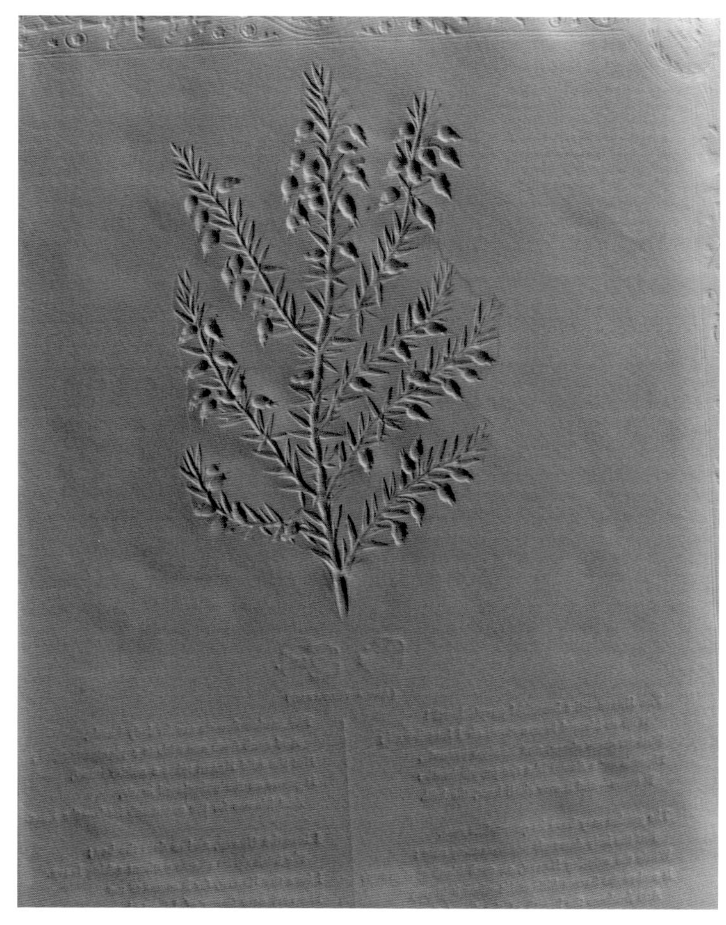

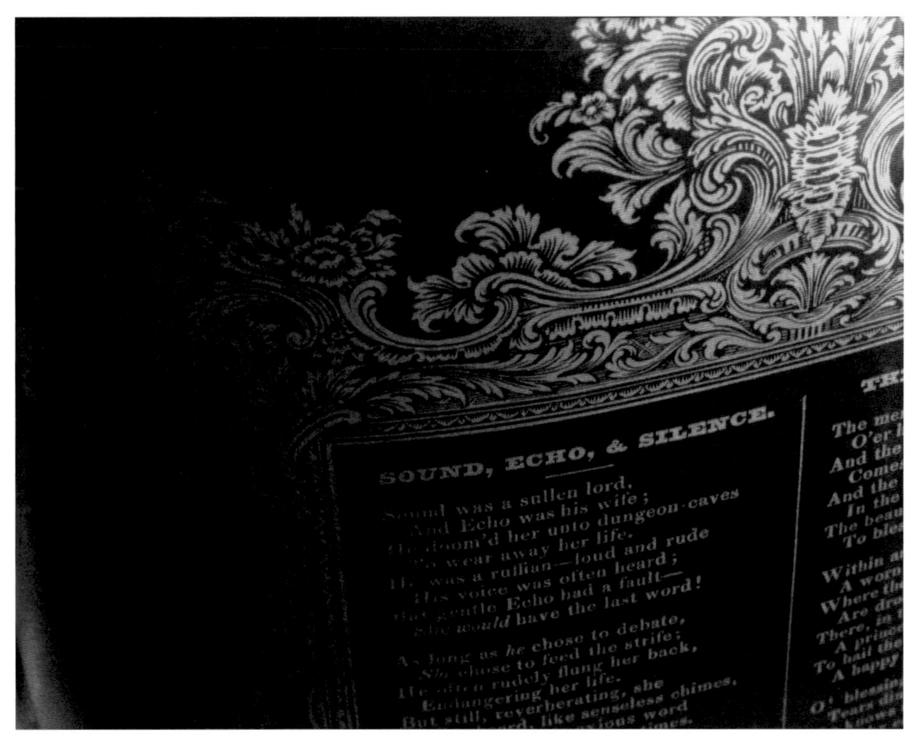
SOUND, ECHO, & SILENCE.

Sound was a sullen lord,
And Echo was his wife;
He doom'd her unto dungeon-caves
To wear away her life.
He was a ruffian—loud and rude
His voice was often heard;
But gentle Echo had a fault—
She would have the last word!

As long as he chose to debate,
She chose to feed the strife;
He often rudely flung her back,
Endangering her life.
But still, reverberating, she
Replied, like senseless chimes,

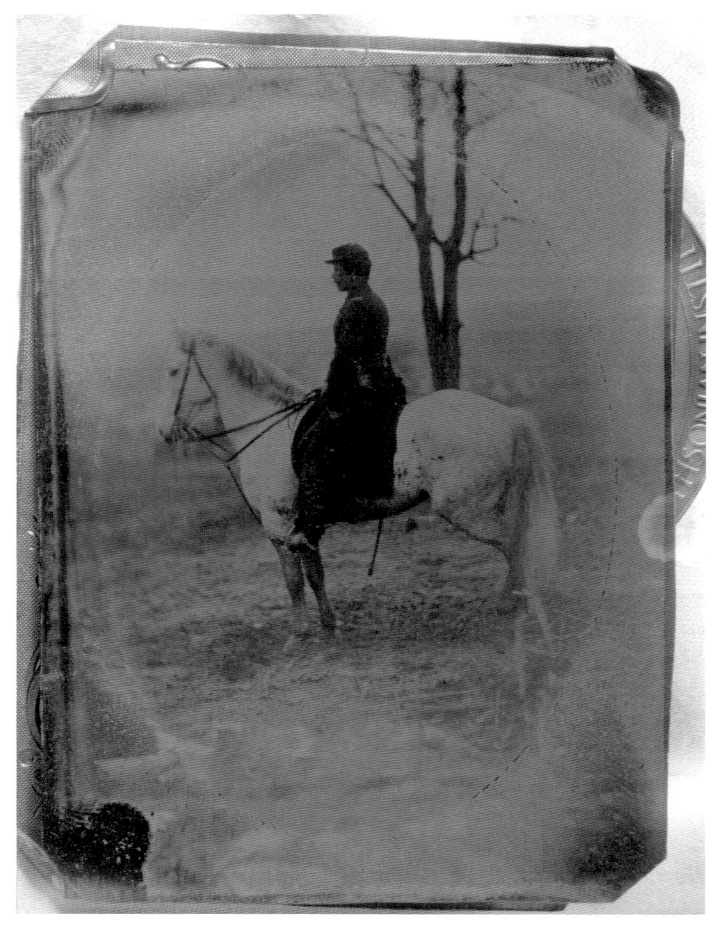

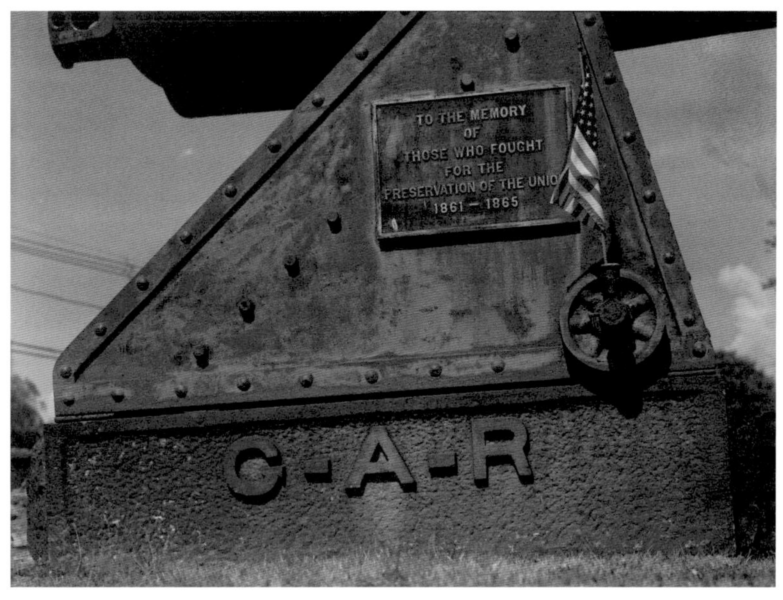

TO THE MEMORY
OF
THOSE WHO FOUGHT
FOR THE
PRESERVATION OF THE UNION
1861 — 1865
G-A-R

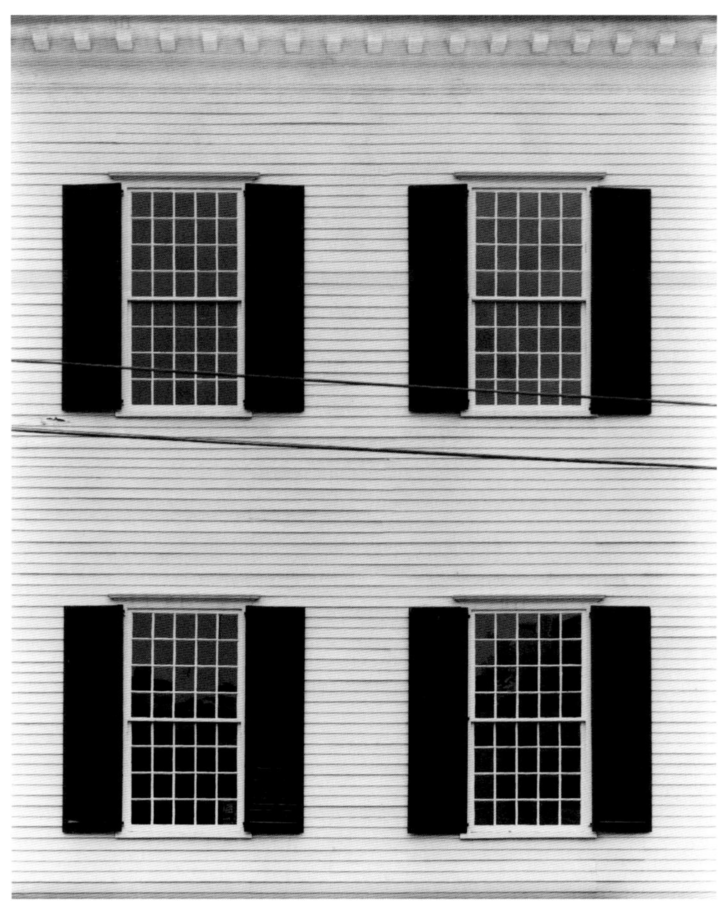

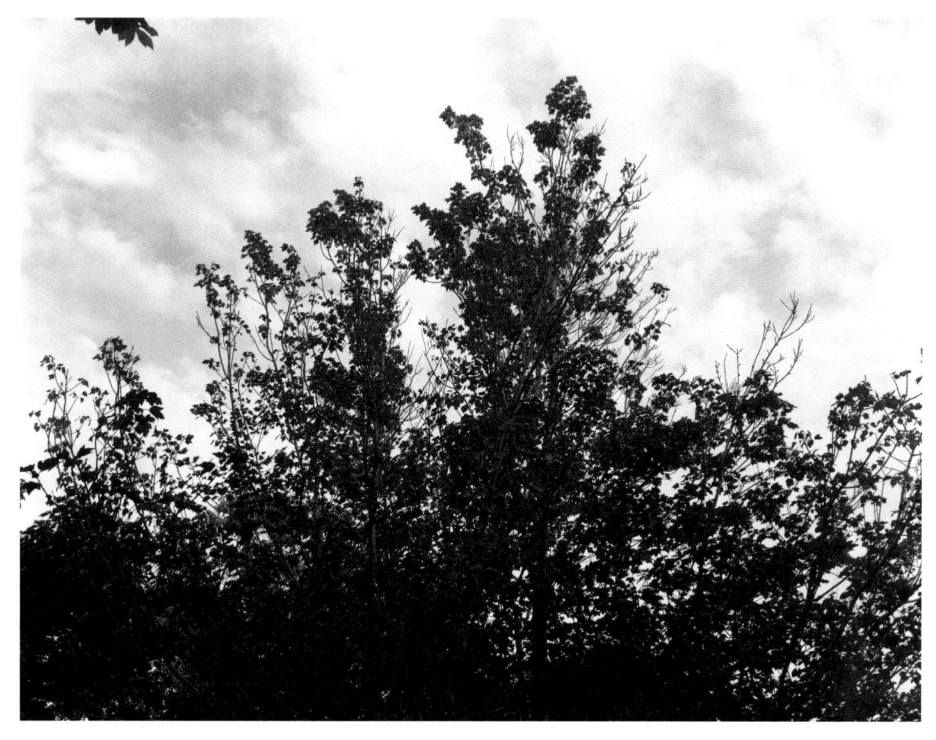

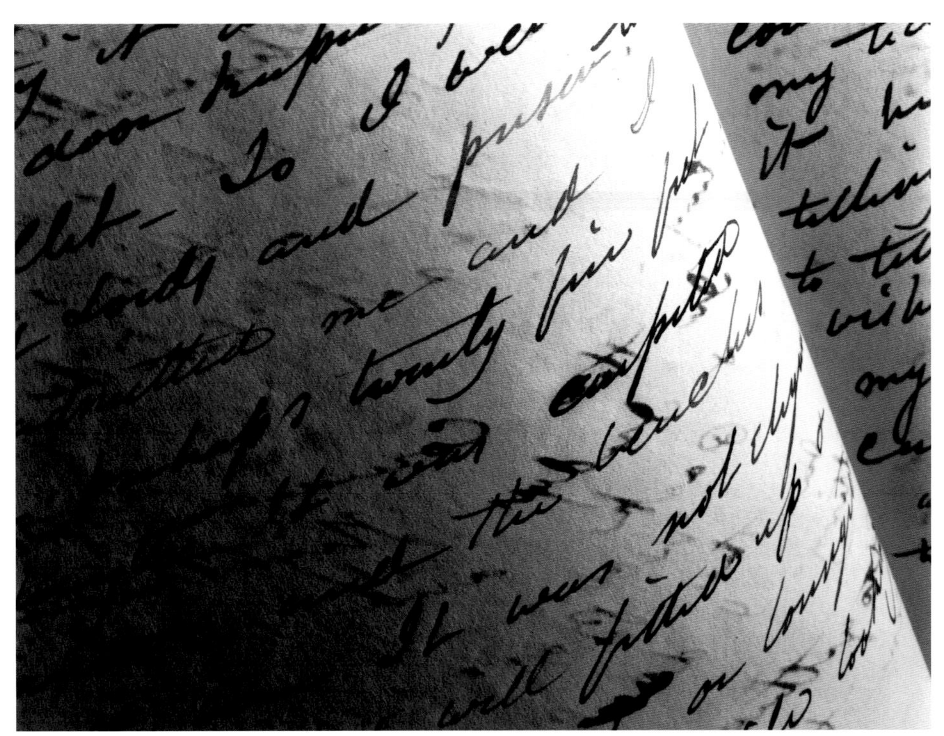

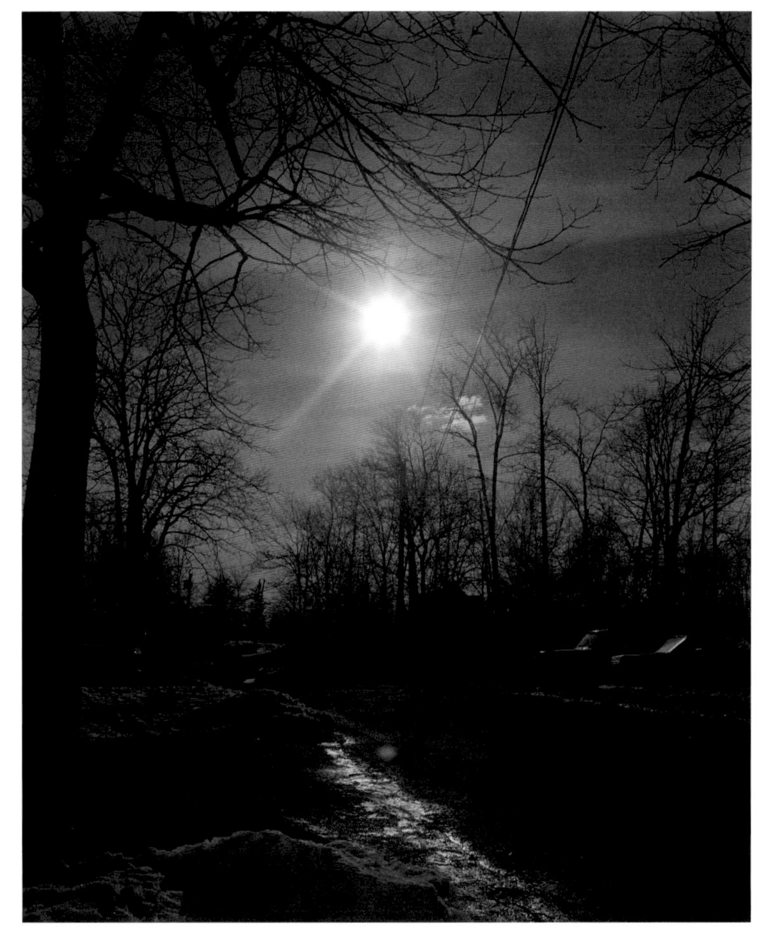

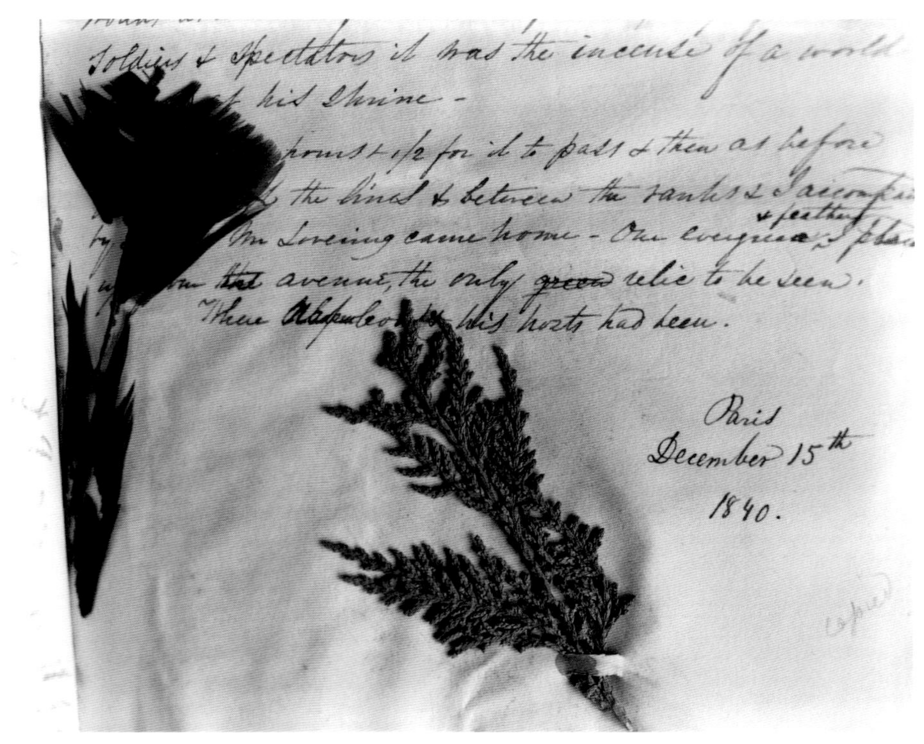
soldiers & spectators it was the incense of a world
at his Shrine —
ground & 1/2 for it to pass & then as before
the lines & between the ranks I accompanied
Mr Loreing came home — One evening
on that avenue, the only green relic to be seen.
Where Napoleon & his hosts had been.
Paris
December 15th
1840.

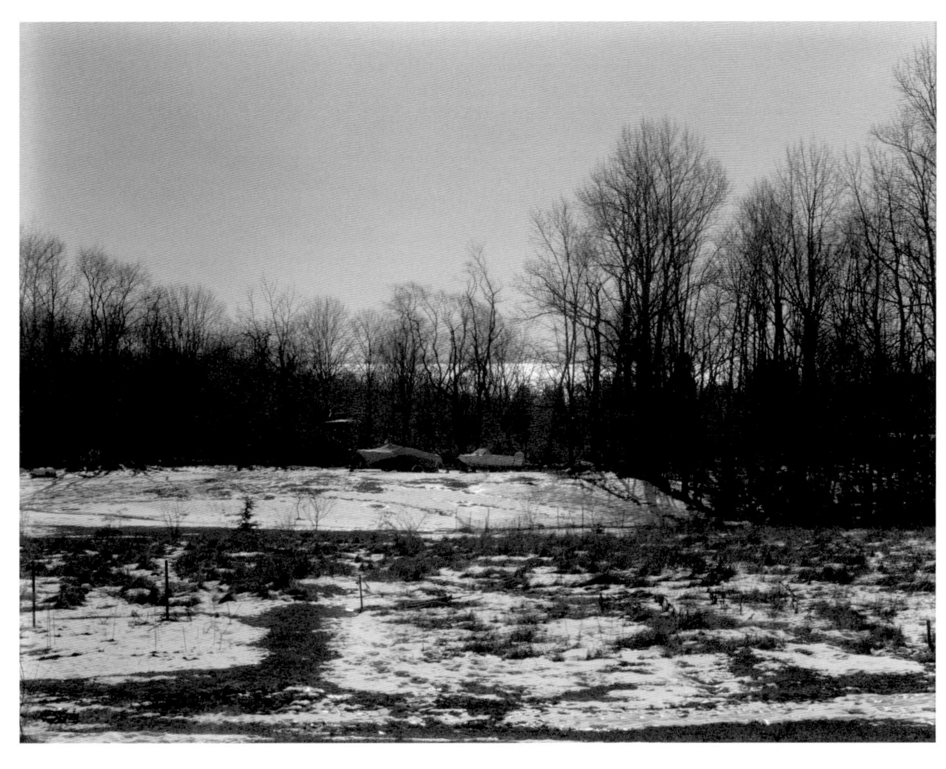

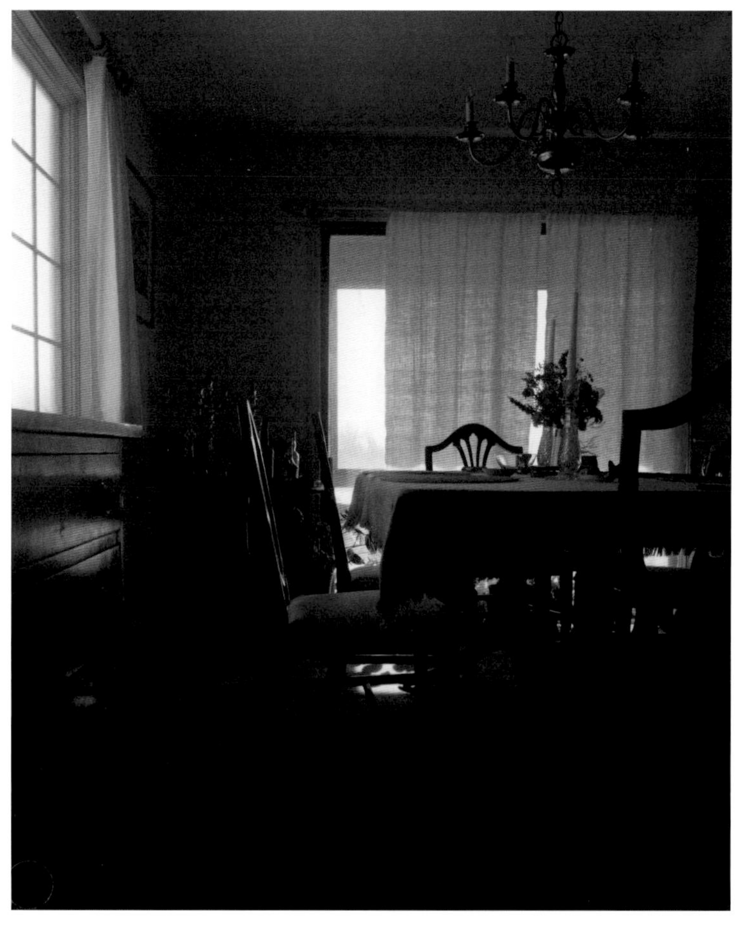

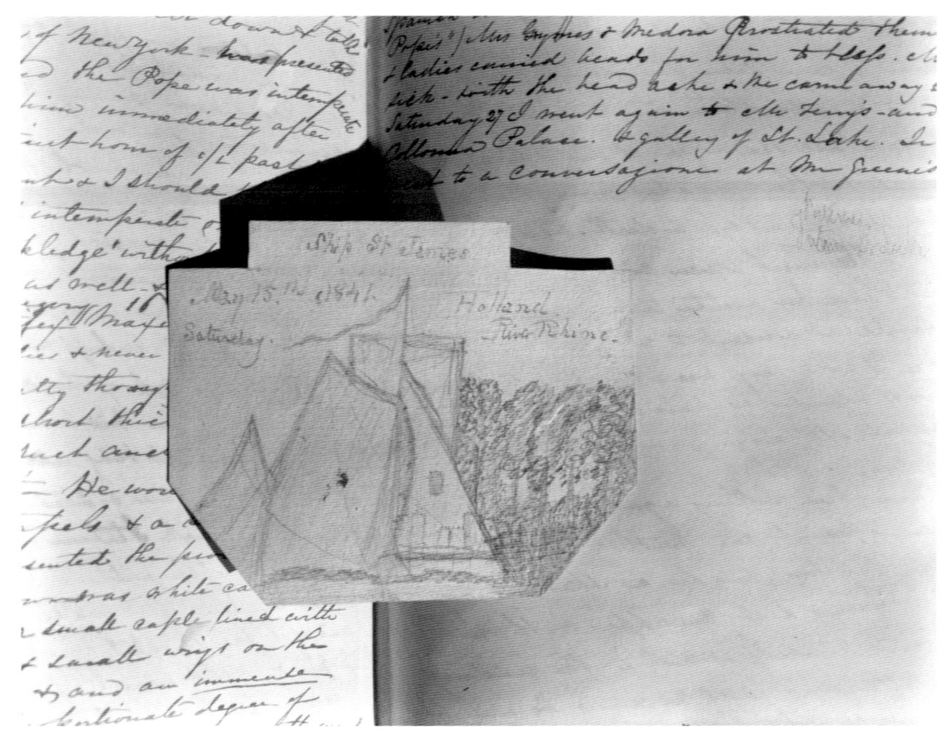
Ship St James
May 15th 1841
Saturday.
Holland
River Rhine.

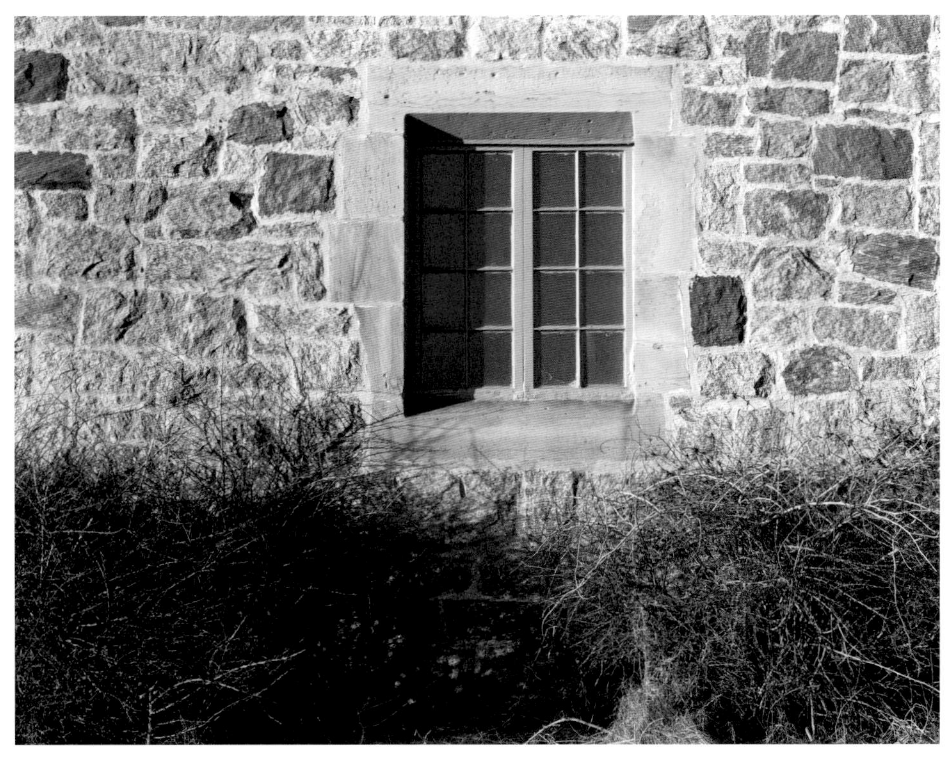

The fresh flower, whence the bee doth honey sip;
These, loves the Sonnetteer, these charm his eye;
And these in tiny lay and language quaint,
With moral saws inwrought he loves to sit and paint.

LOVE.

Oh Love, it is a wond'rous thing, a thing of hopes and fears,
Starts into birth with bounding joy, or springs to life in tears!
Gleams like the morning's rising sun, as beautiful, as bright;
Or beams a solitary star, amid the gloom of night;—
A summer-sky without a cloud, a winter night of storms;
A fadeless flower upon life's waste, no blight or blast deforms.

Oh Love! it is a happy thing, when those we love are nigh,
When on us beams the heavenly glance of *one* bright azure eye;
When *one* sweet voice with silvery tone can bid the heart be gay,
When *one* sweet smile can chase the gloom from sorrow's brow away,
When *one* heart beats in unison all tremblingly with ours,
This, only this, can make the world a paradise of flowers!—

Oh Love it is a mournful thing when those we love are gone,
Leaving us in this desert world all sorrowful and lone,
When Hope can throw no joyous rays upon the future scene,
And memory only droops her head to weep for what hath been;
'Tis then that love becomes a thing of doubtings and of fears;
A flower, whose zephyr is a sigh, whose dew-drops, beauty's tears!

Oh Love! it is a holy thing, when faith with stedfast eye,
Looks for a world where friends shall meet in happier realms on high;
Where, when the fame of earth shall sink to darkness and decay,
The spirit soars on Angel wings beyond the stars away.
And 'tis this hope, and this alone, that makes Love's holy flame,
In storm and calm, in grief and joy, for ever burn the same.

J. F. Clarke.

THE NUN.

And this,
Like antle
But soft a
Why is it
Gracefull
Wet with
Along the
When ga
That pro
Bent dow

For from
Such flatt
Although
Pre-emin
But a sev
In every
Stamped
A simple
That mu
To love

A laurel
A heavie
But wou
The chil
That mi
A multi
But this
Records
And fool
I bore it

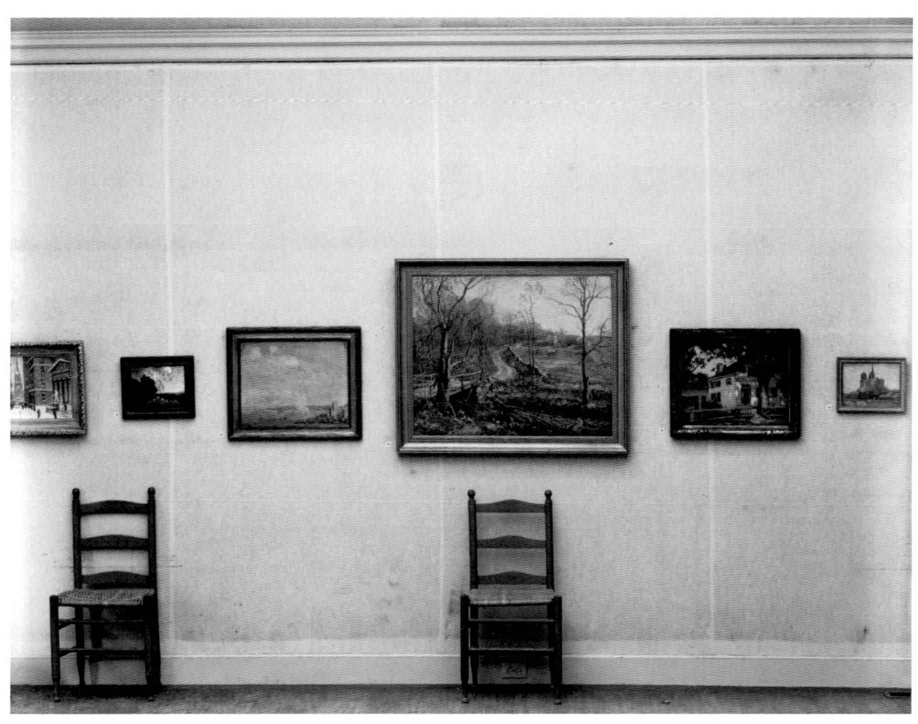

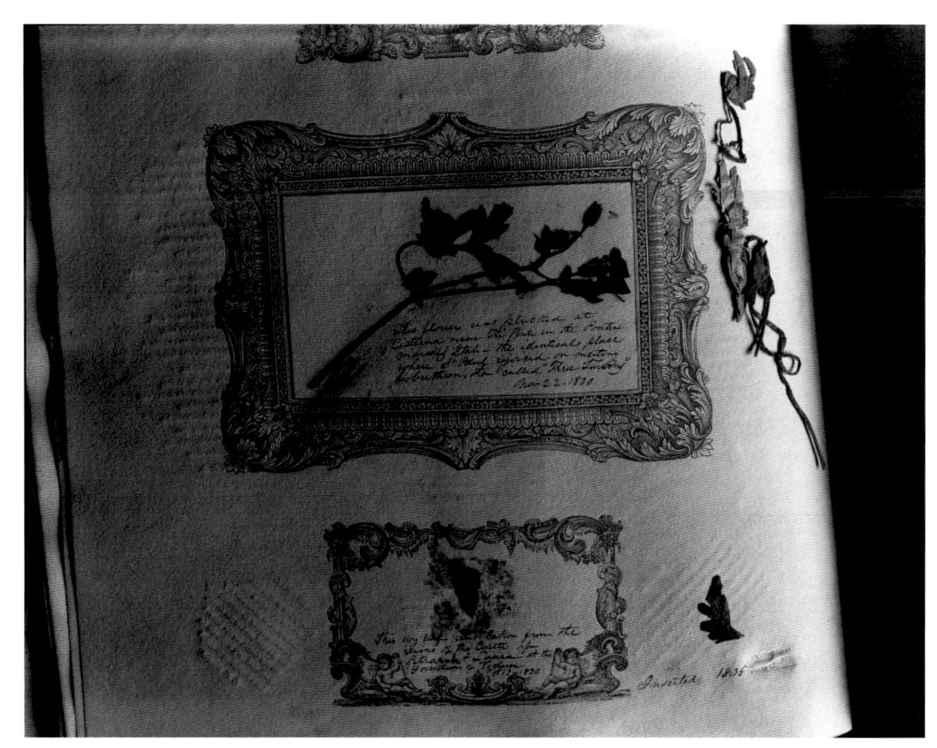

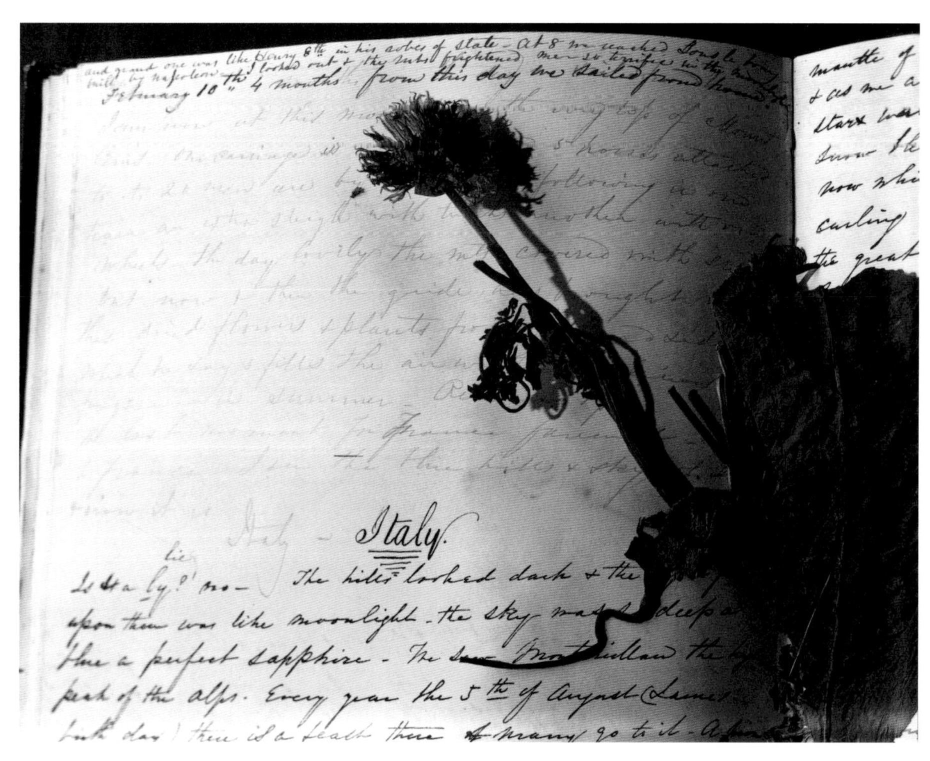

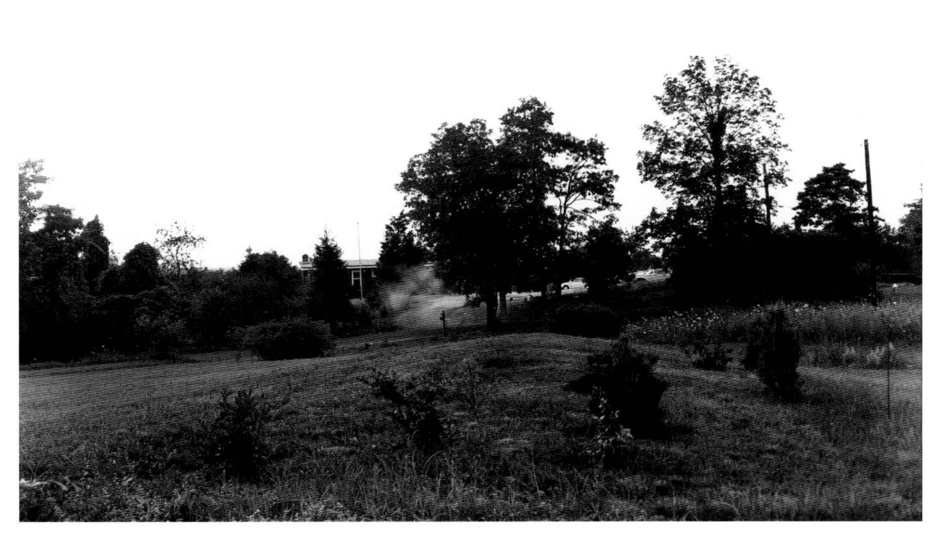

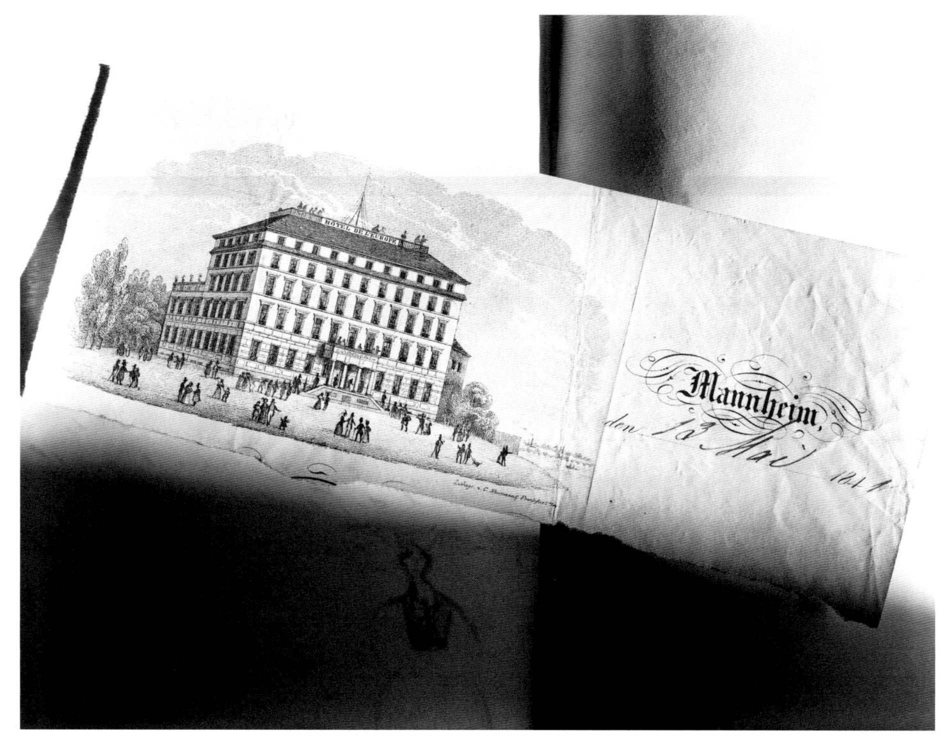

43

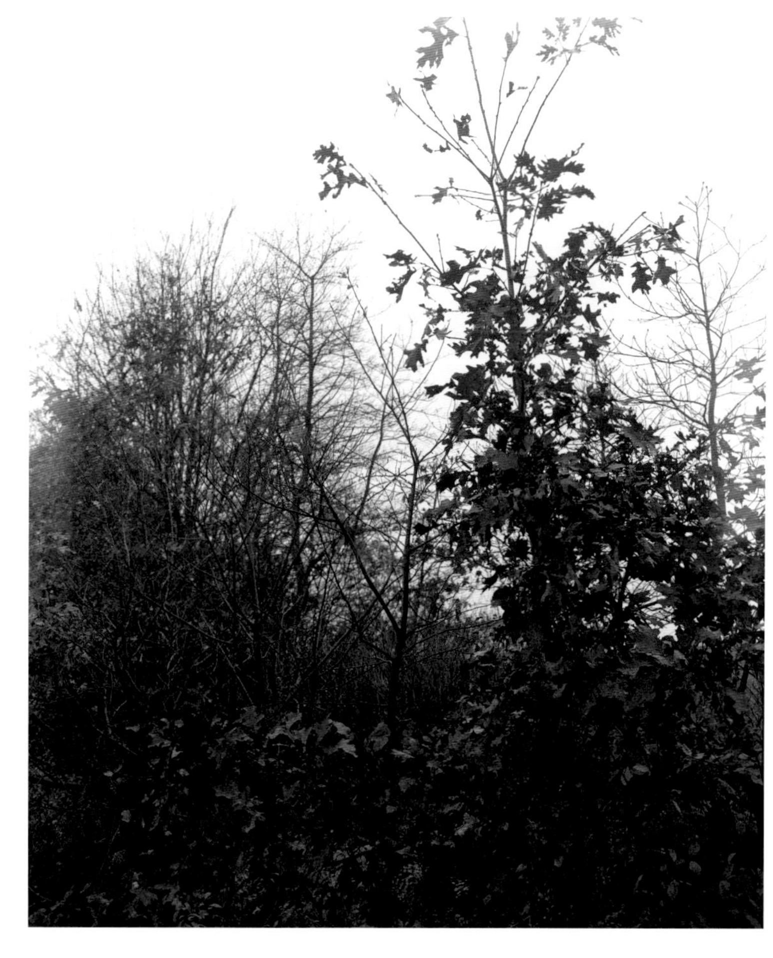

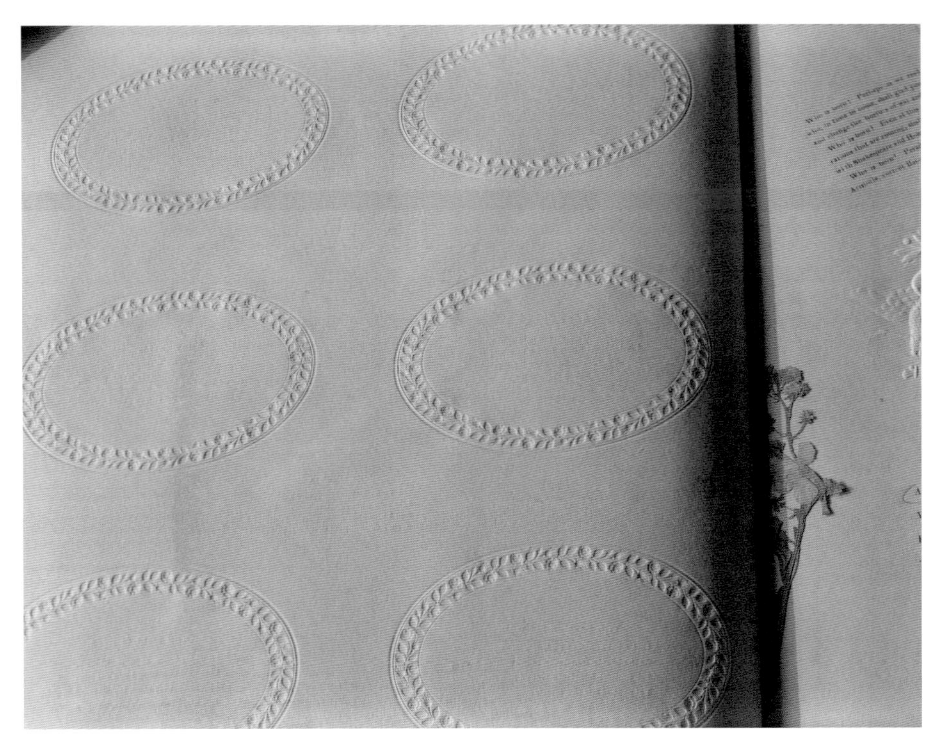

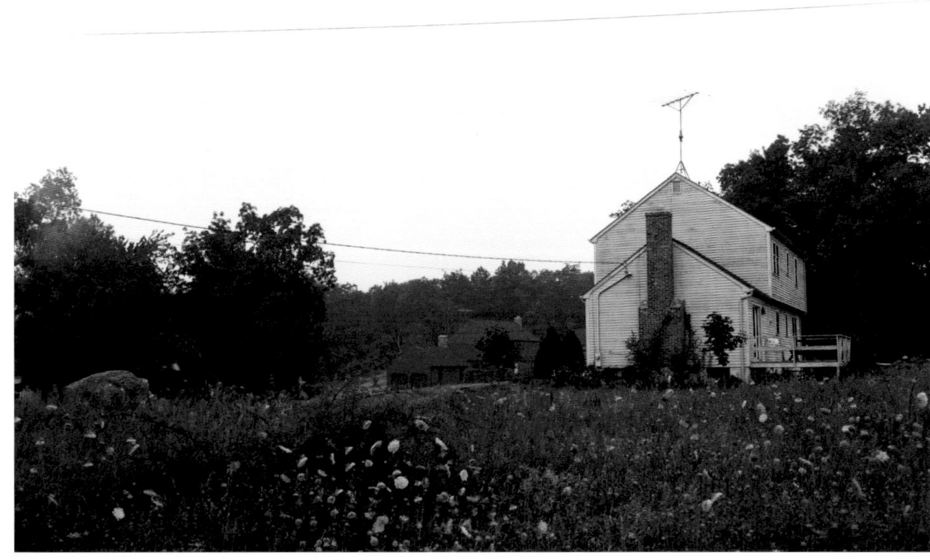

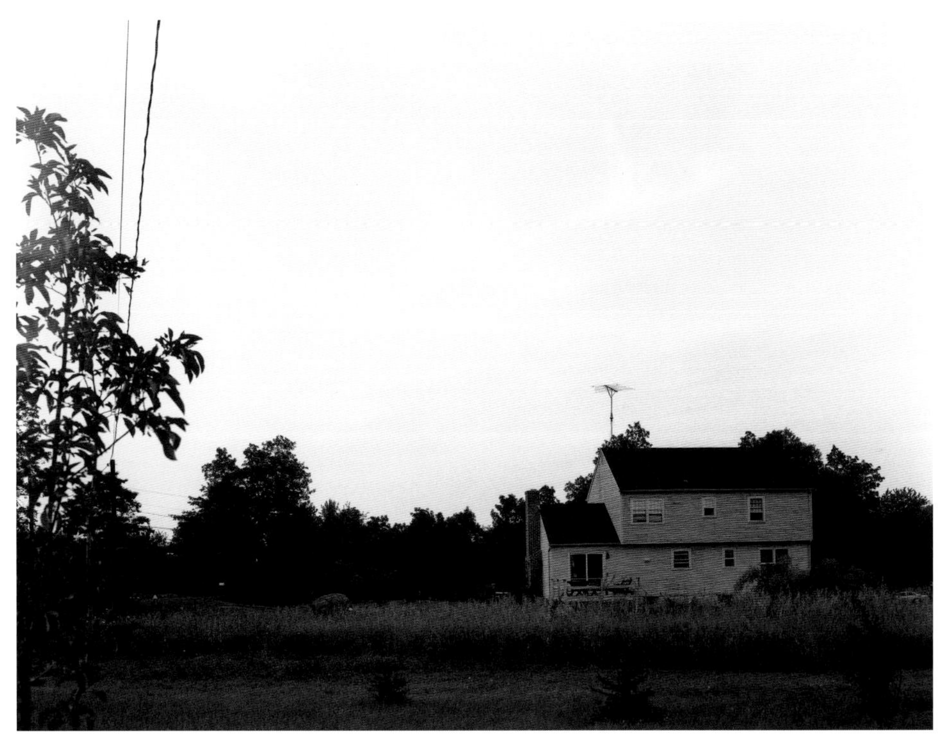

arest Shrubs & flowe
Enchanting for occasionally the whol
d by a smile from the sun — Cowslip Gree
y word but the latter was the favourite resid
plucked this ivy leaf from the bower whi
it. —

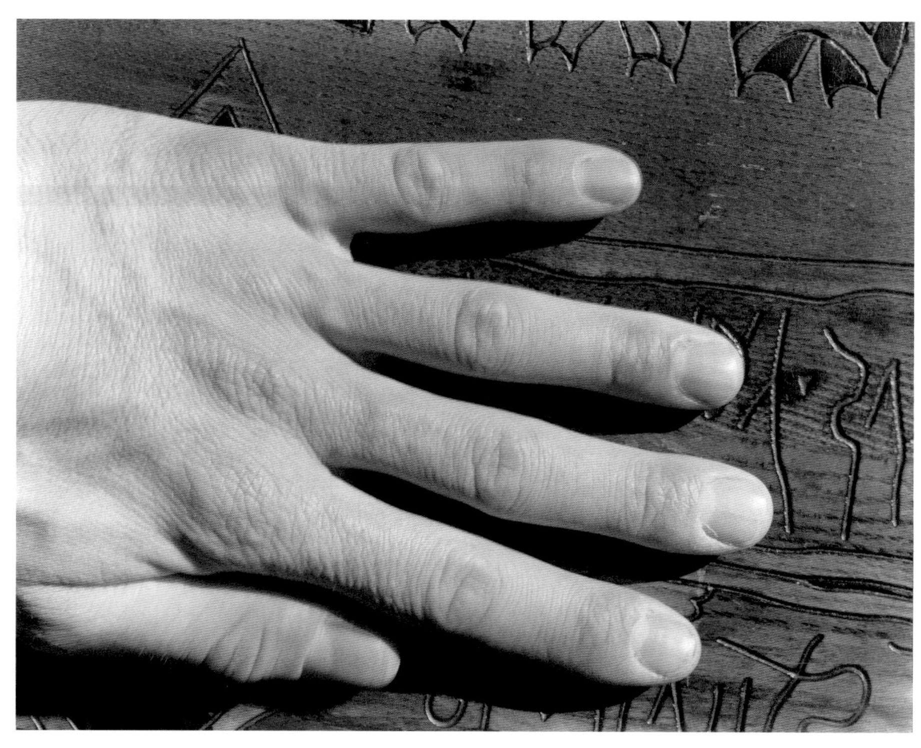

Volume 3rd.

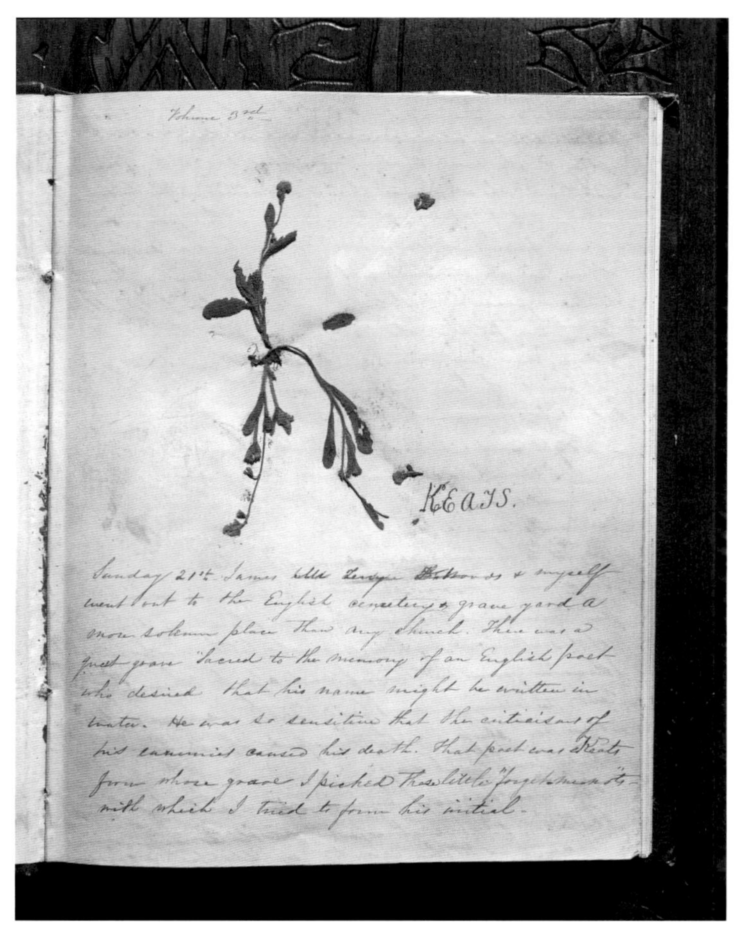

Sunday 21st James Udd George Bedmonds & myself
went out to the English cemetery & grave yard A
more solemn place than any Church. There was a
quiet grave "Sacred to the memory of an English poet
who desired that his name might be written in
water. He was so sensitive that the criticisms of
his enemies caused his death. That poet was Keats
from whose grave I picked these little "forget-me-nots"
with which I tried to form his initial.

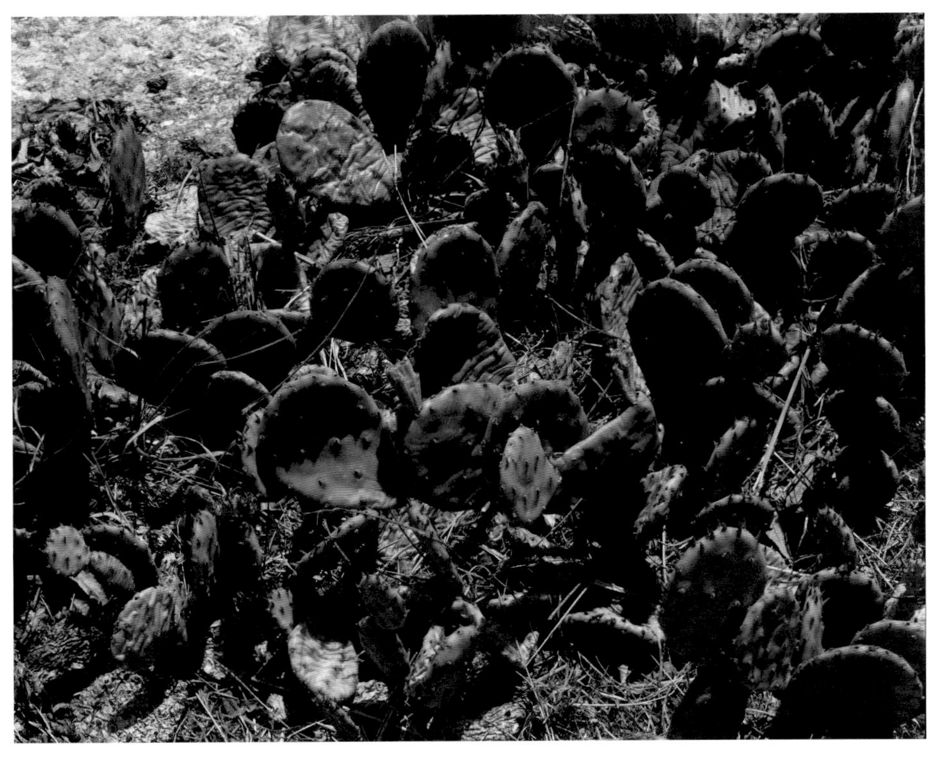

was built by Catherine de Medicis (a

having been erected on a piece

to the manufacture of tiles). Louis

establishment. In one side of this pa

the Carousel & the Louvre which R

appa extends shall be equally gra

intervening buildings & then it wil

Palace & the whole will form the most spl

appa

side are

lleries

contains

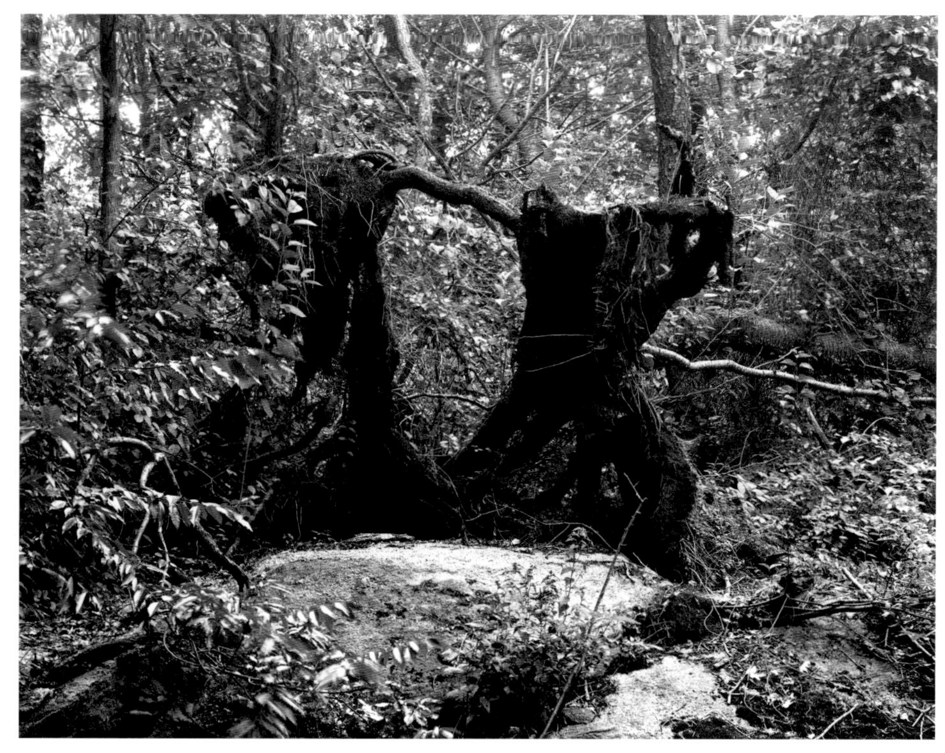

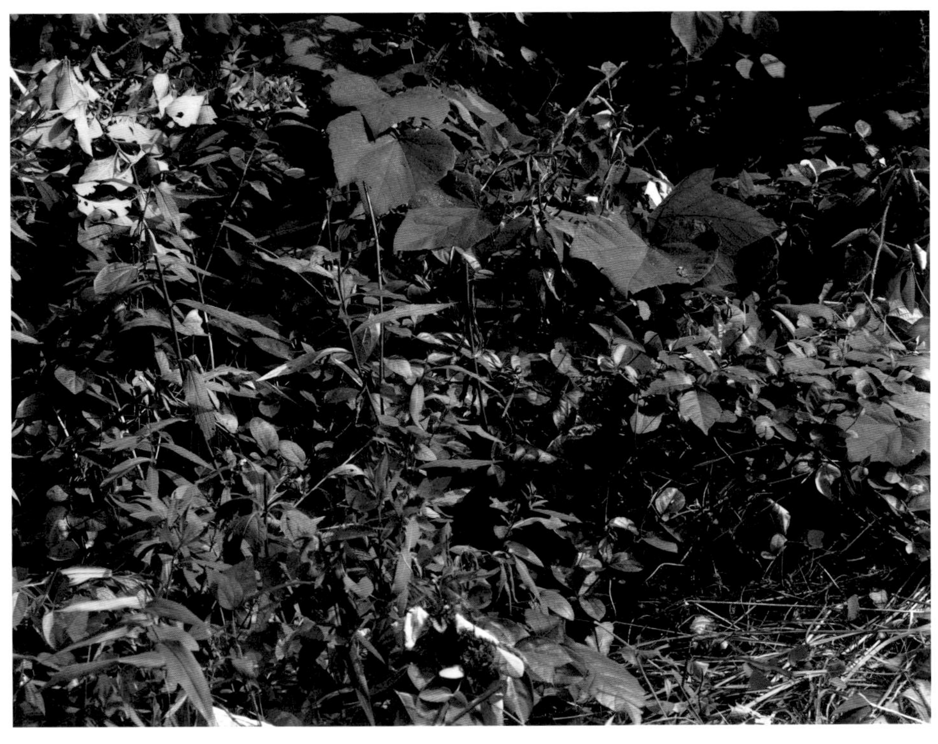

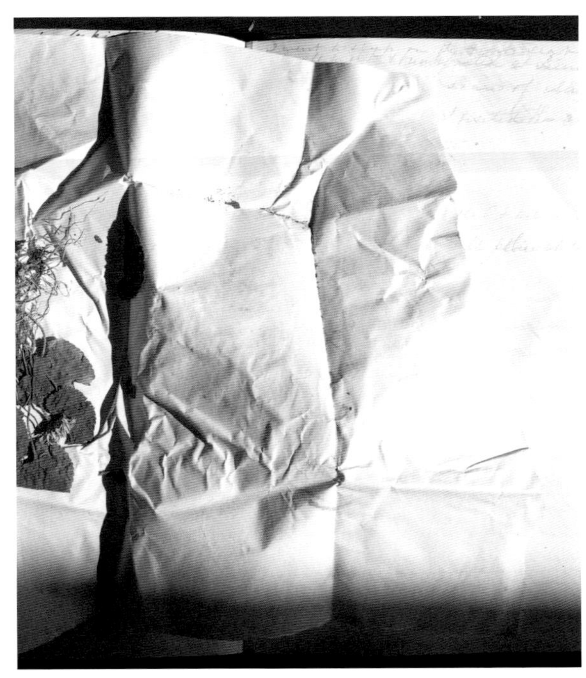

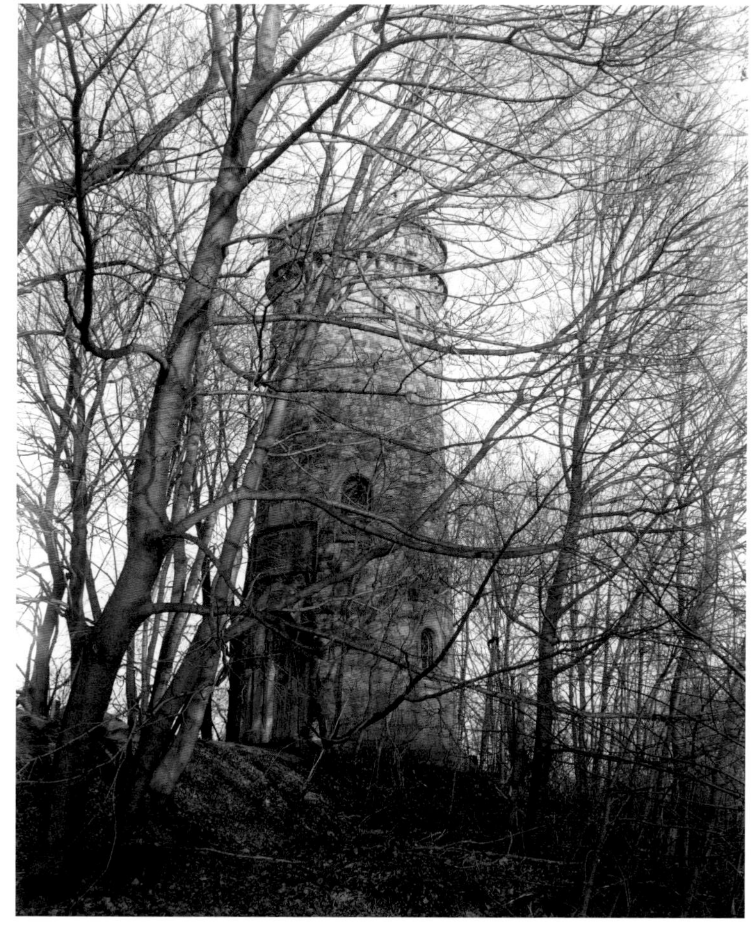

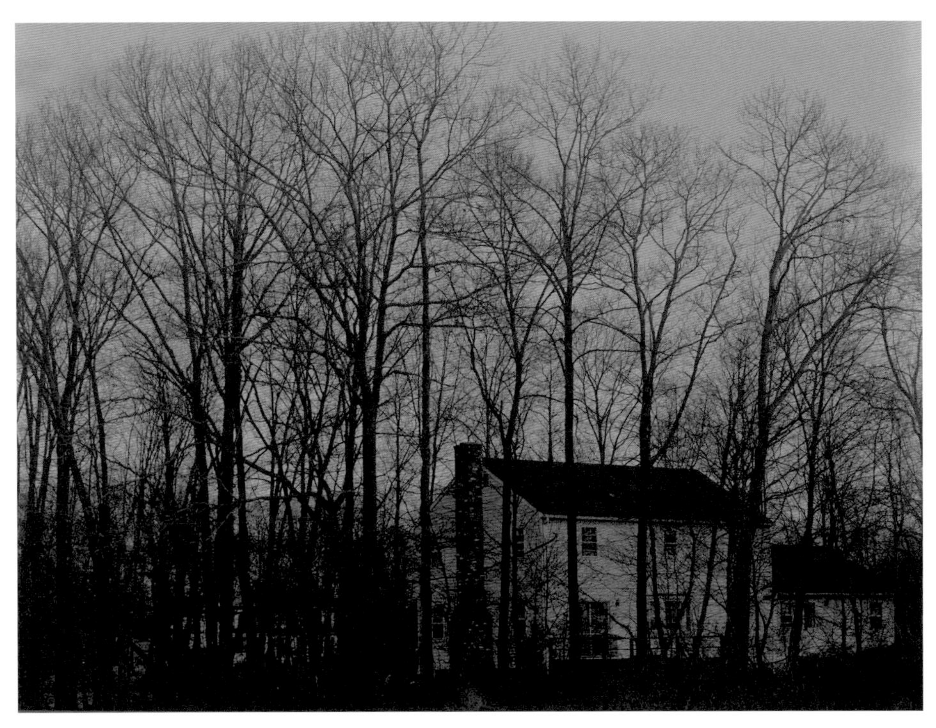

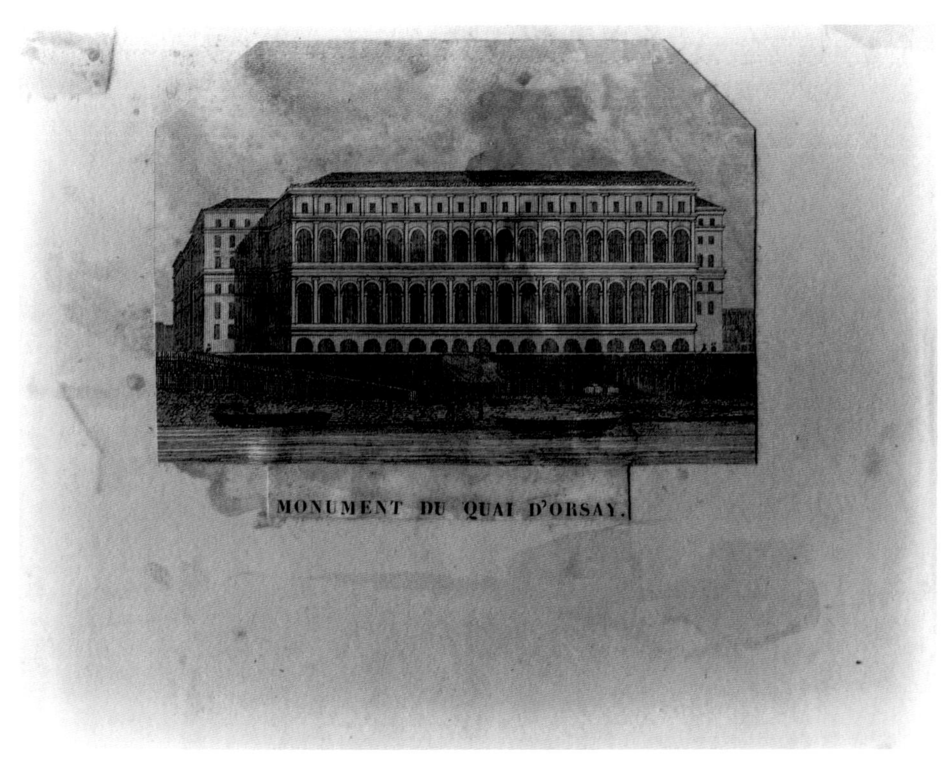

MONUMENT DU QUAI D'ORSAY.

...was

...e said and stretched out her hand
Mrs Dixon" I am glad to see you —
's she made me fill a large
the first time I had sat down
young officer came & asked me in
th kind & I said "Avec plaisir for
had desired me not to waltz
...ame to see Mrs Sigourney & th...
...th said I must go & the music
...led me off — "Is me valse pas bi...
..., but he did and away we whirled
...lished floor. James, Mrs. Sigourney &
...d in Seth!) looked on. I was a part of the
the floor & Mrs S. Exclaimed "Just look
...ee the little fairy" Why do see the little
"" Miss Gardiner thought me a sylph —
...t. Miss G. told the Nicolls she thought
...ustry couple she ever saw: he Le
...so interesting! He was one of the
...tlemen there with his golden cu...

the 19th
...ells came & taking...
...m it is time for sober peopl...
i past 12", Mrs S. rose with...
...he evening who passed the da...
with...and had met me it the
...had not spoken came up f...

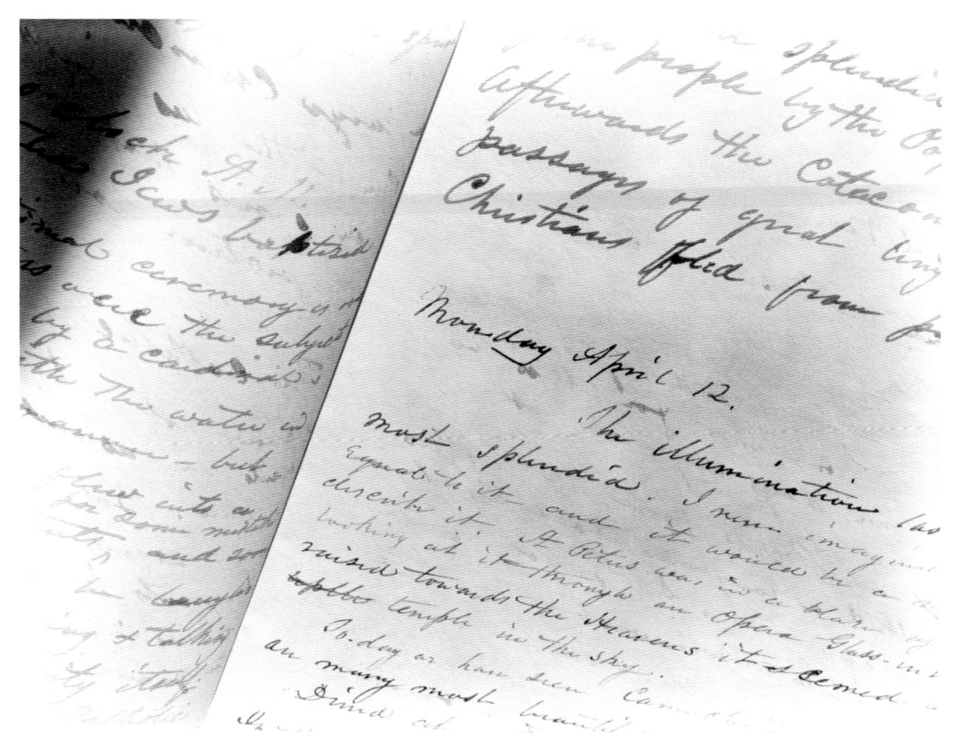

… of great … Christians fled from …

Monday April 12.

The illumination las[t] … most splendid. I never imagine[d] … equal to it — and … describe it. St Peters was in a blaze … looking at it through an Opera Glass — … raised towards the Heavens it seemed … temple in the sky. … To-day or have seen Camel[s] … many most beautiful … dined at …

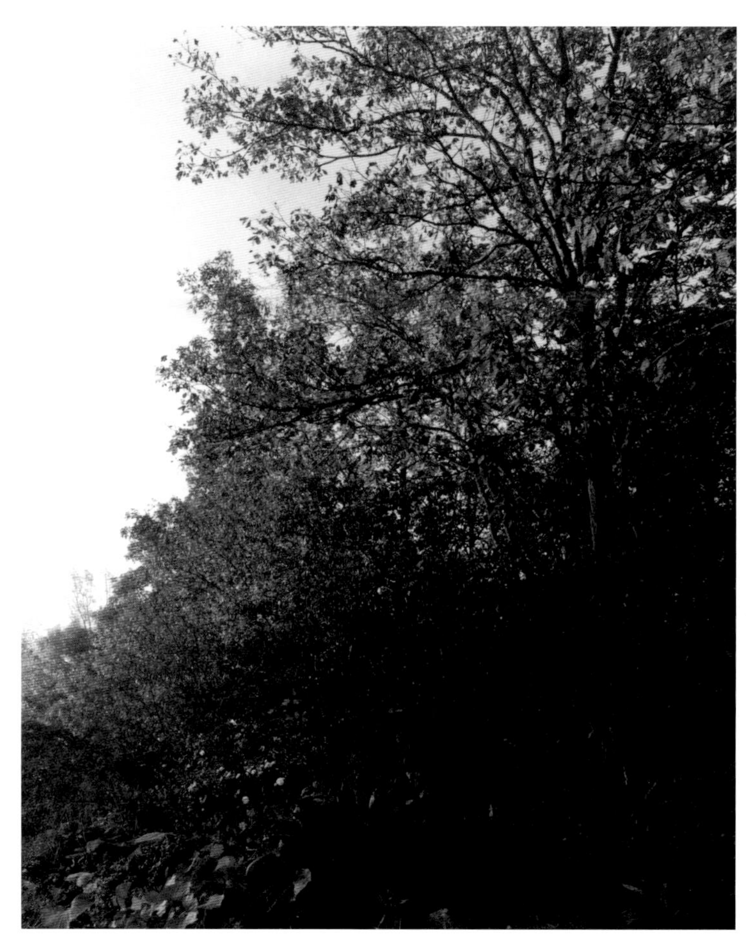

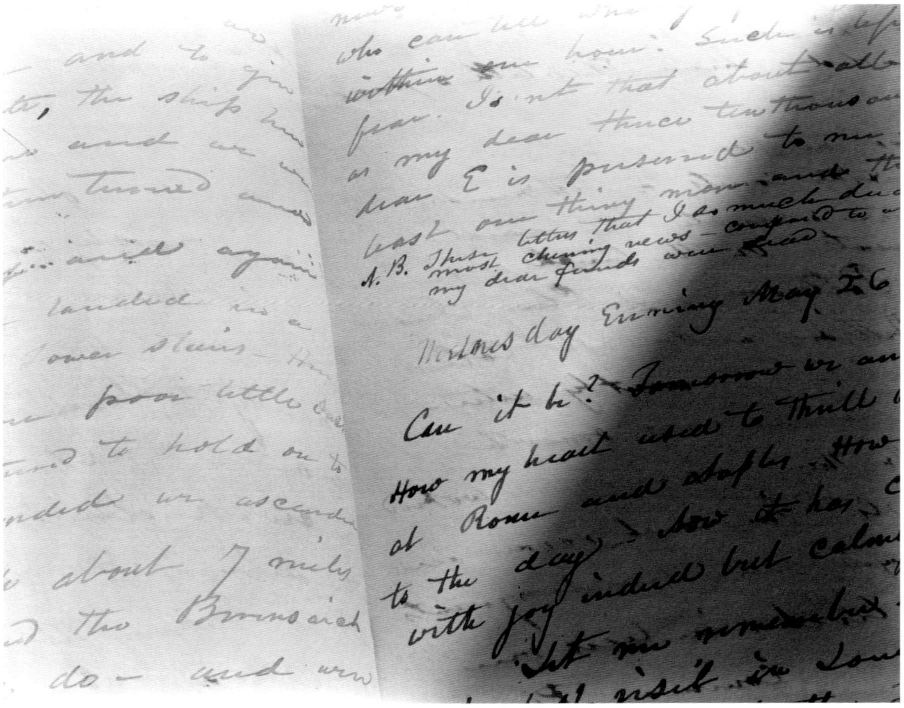

who can tell who / within one hour! Such is life
fear. Is'nt that about all
as my dear three ten thousan[d]
dear E is preserved to me
least one thing more and th[e]
A. B. These letters that I so much d[ue]
most cheering news — compared to
my dear friends were [   ]

Wednesday Evening May 26

Can it be? Tomorrow we an[d]
How my heart used to thrill
at Rome and abroad. How
to the day. Now it has
with joy indeed but calm
Let me remember
[   ] visit in Lon[don]

...ackets trimmed with
...aging mothers — anxious
...us dangling — red fa...
& Every scene that passed before
...cession of Novels and
...s & at last all rose &
...ly room enough to pass
...American Ladies distinguish
...pass around to our three
...crowded to suffocation
...out asked the name &
talking to one would ask
...came to me & the King
...son". — The King bowed ...
...all the color forsake my

from what part — t...
I said — "Oh — Connec...
it is a charming cou...
You intend passing
You may enjoy it" —
went and as he wen...
— To the next being y...
not speak — but to the...
& said those were ...
&c. &c., I tried to r...
Scarlett — Gold & di...
with White Plumes.
...our Equilibrium and
"La Reine"! caused us
to our full answer

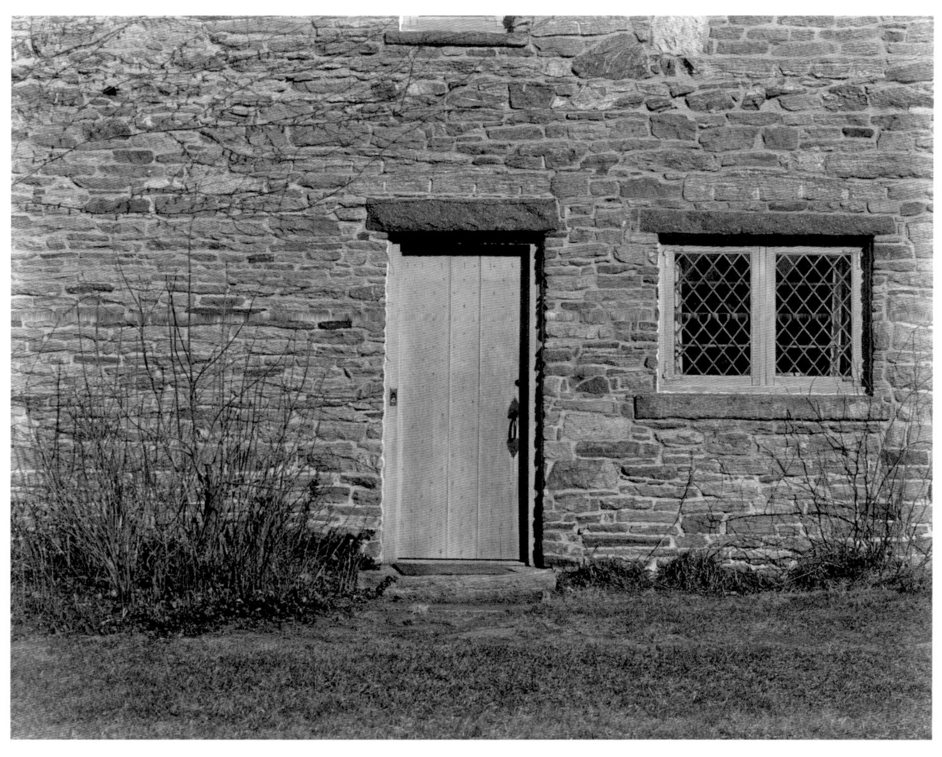

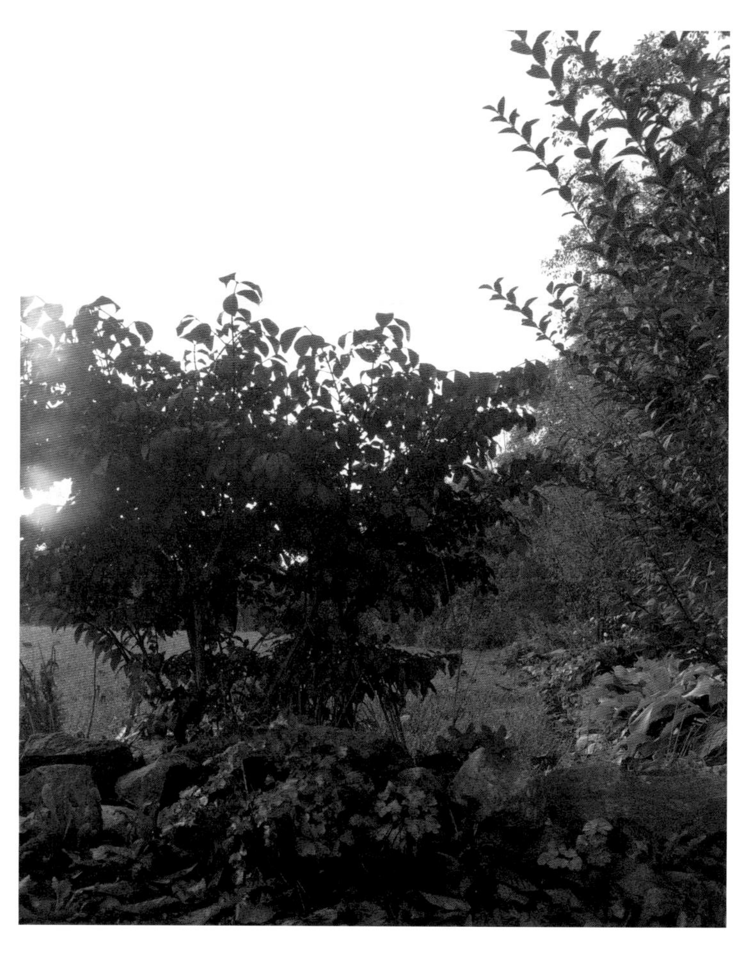

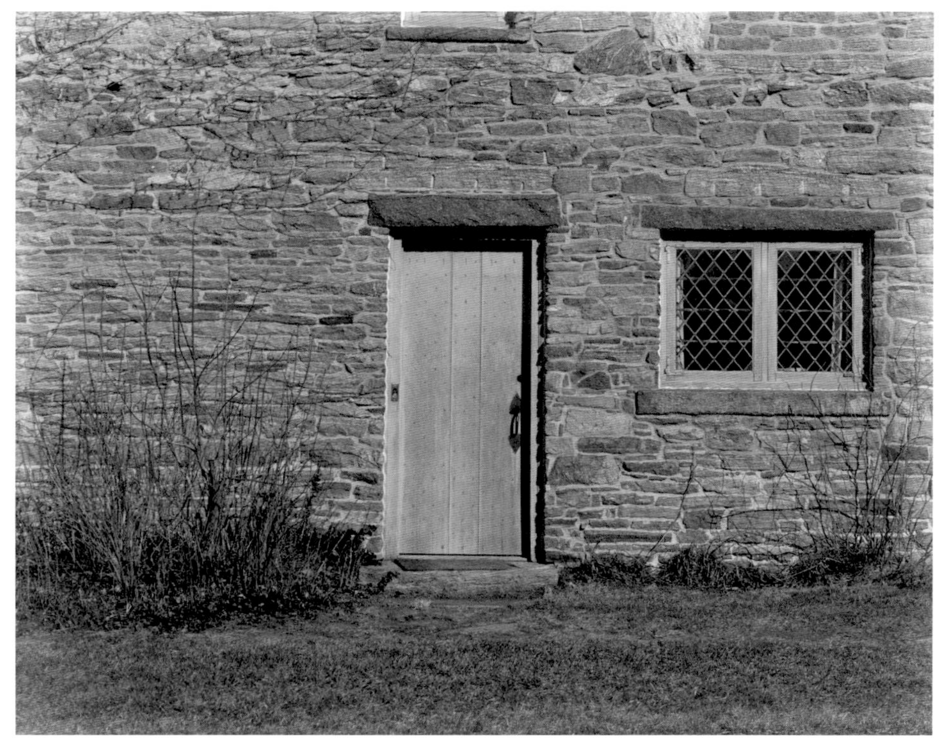

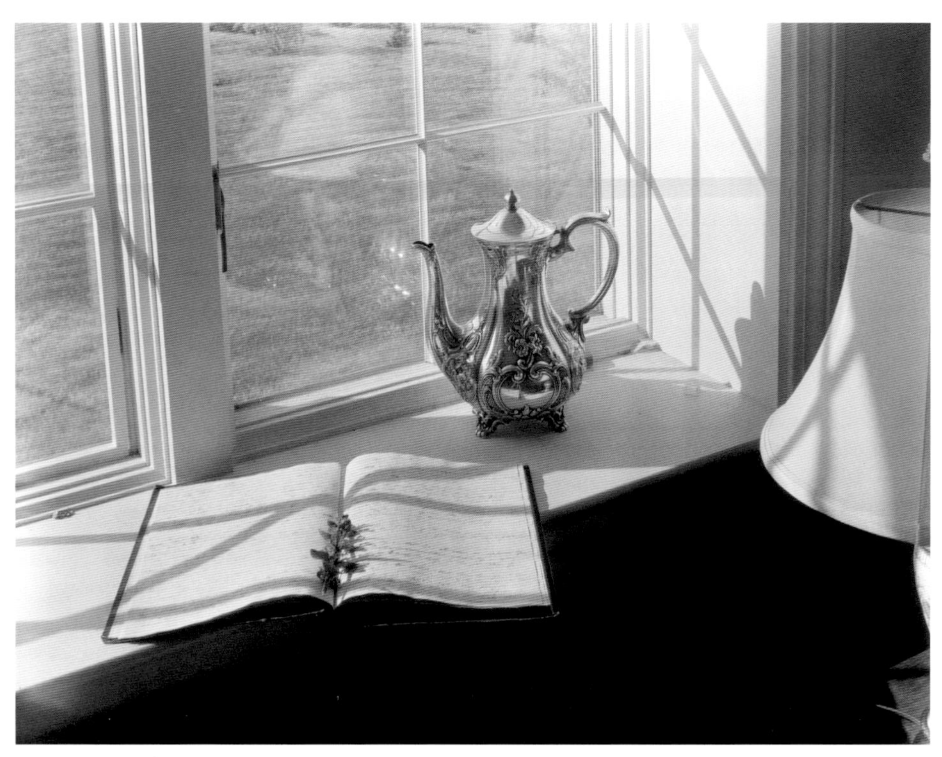

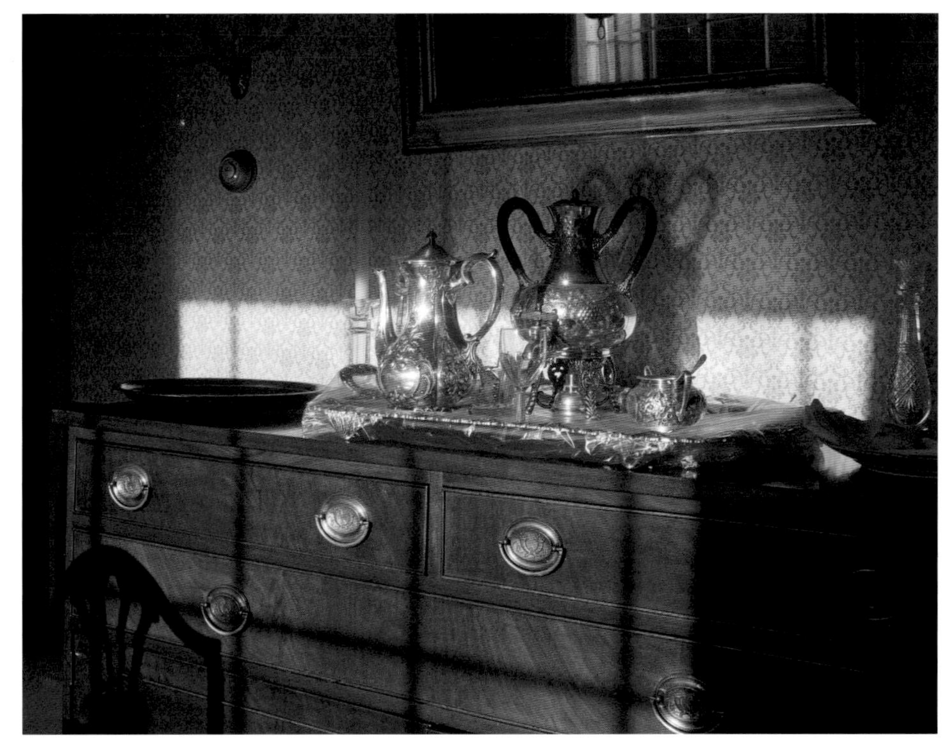

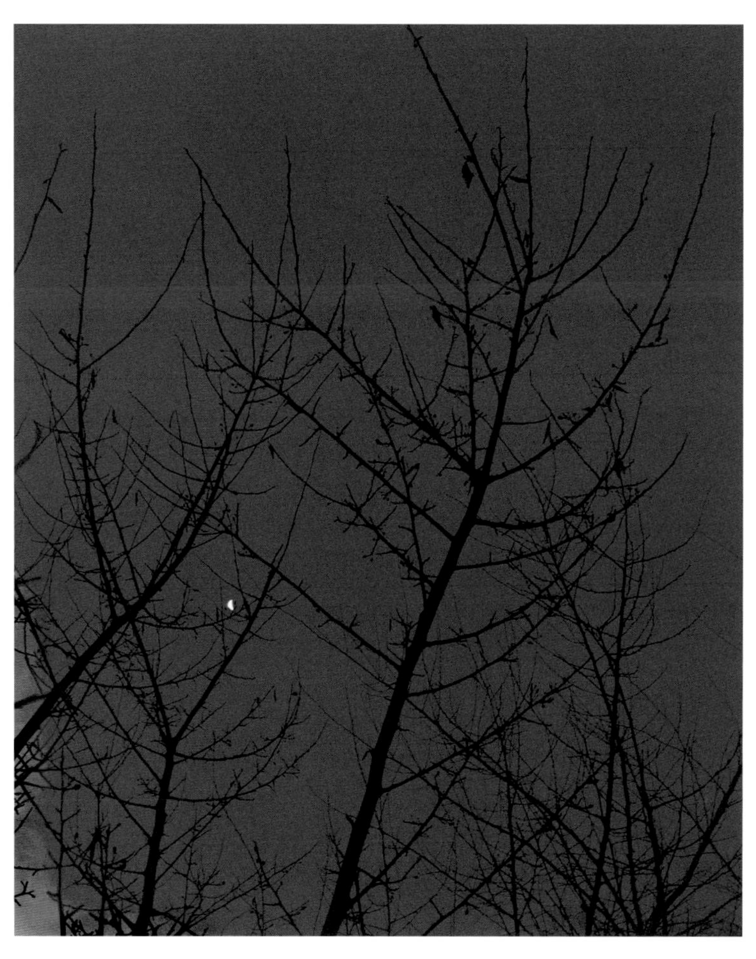

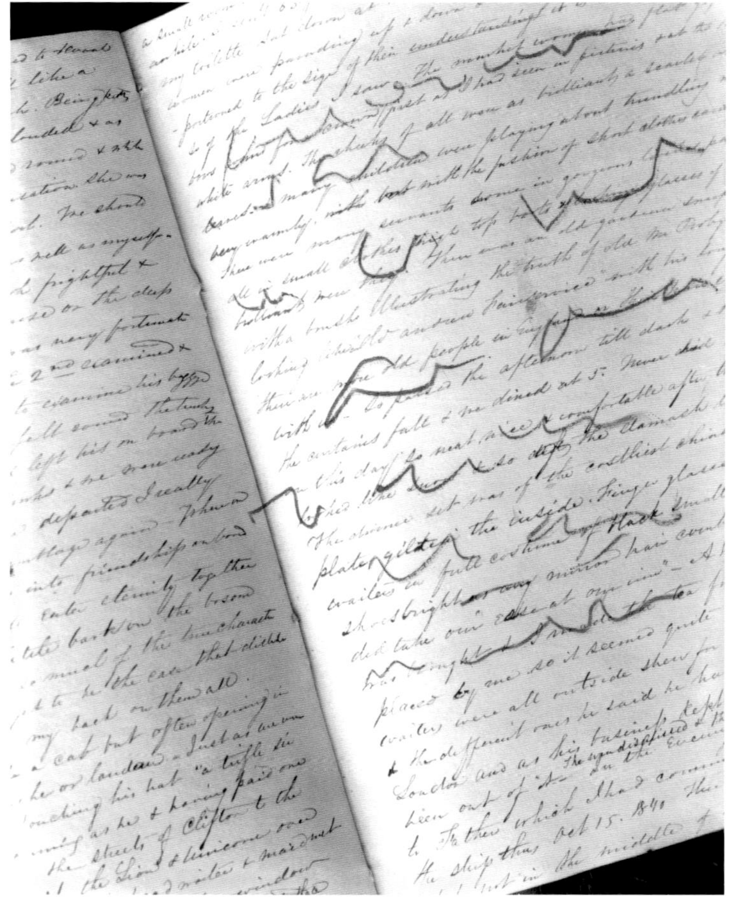

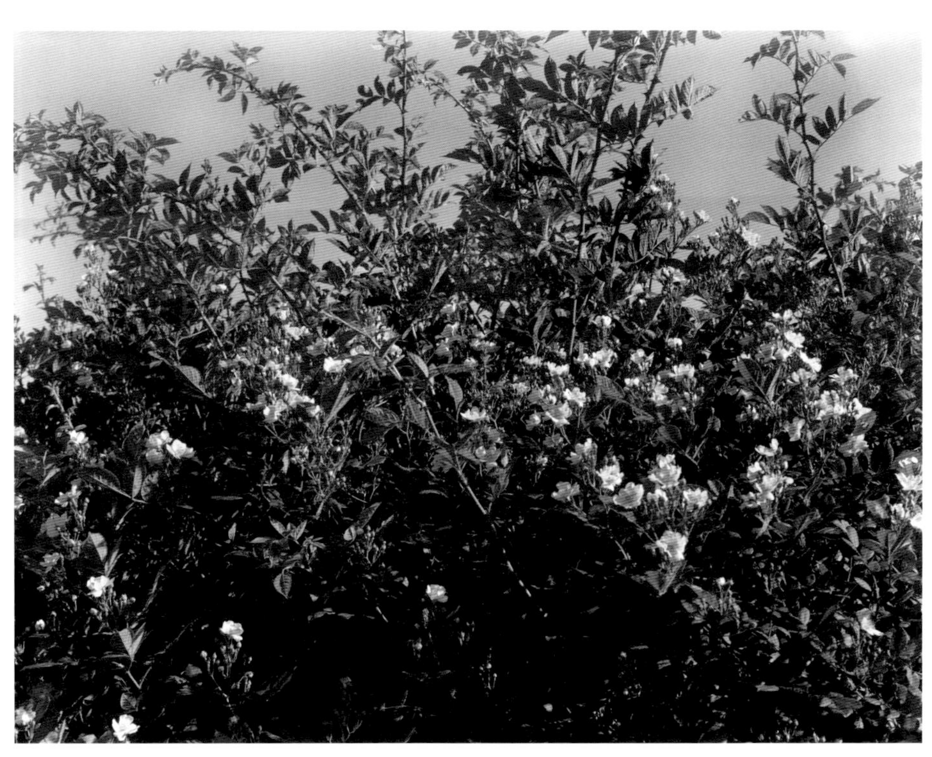

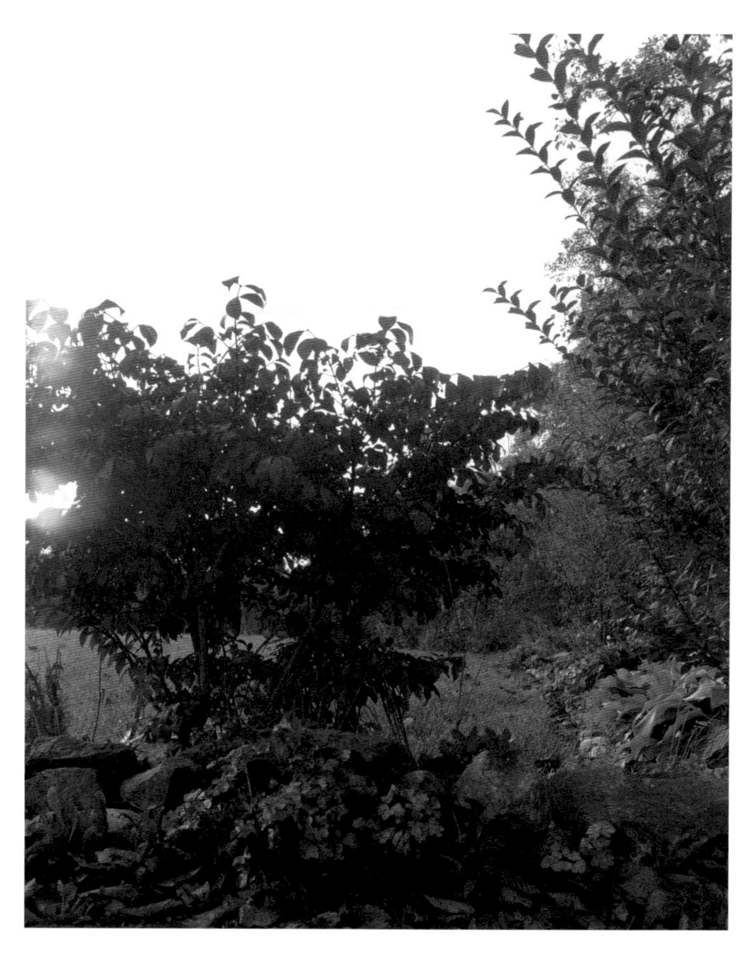

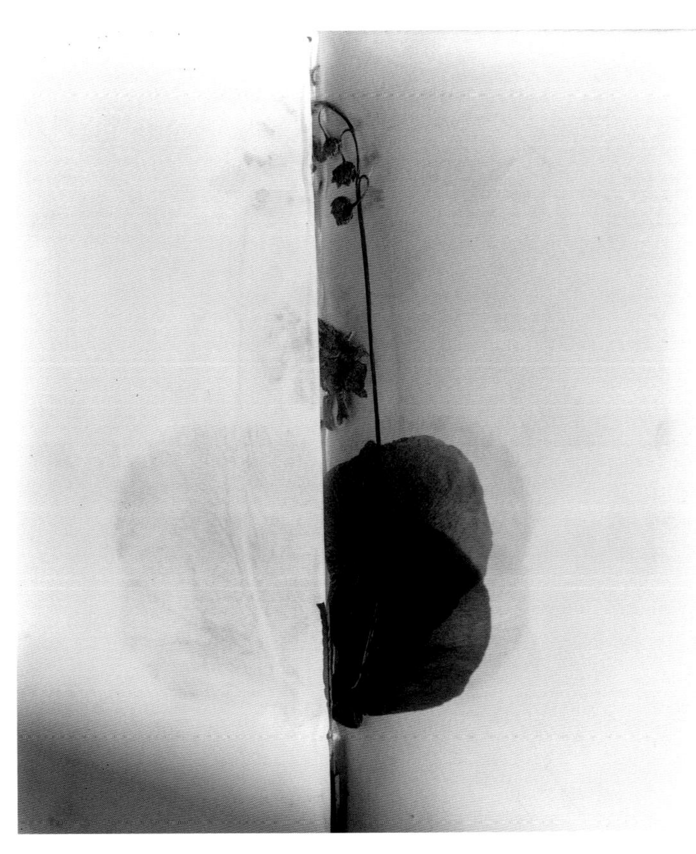

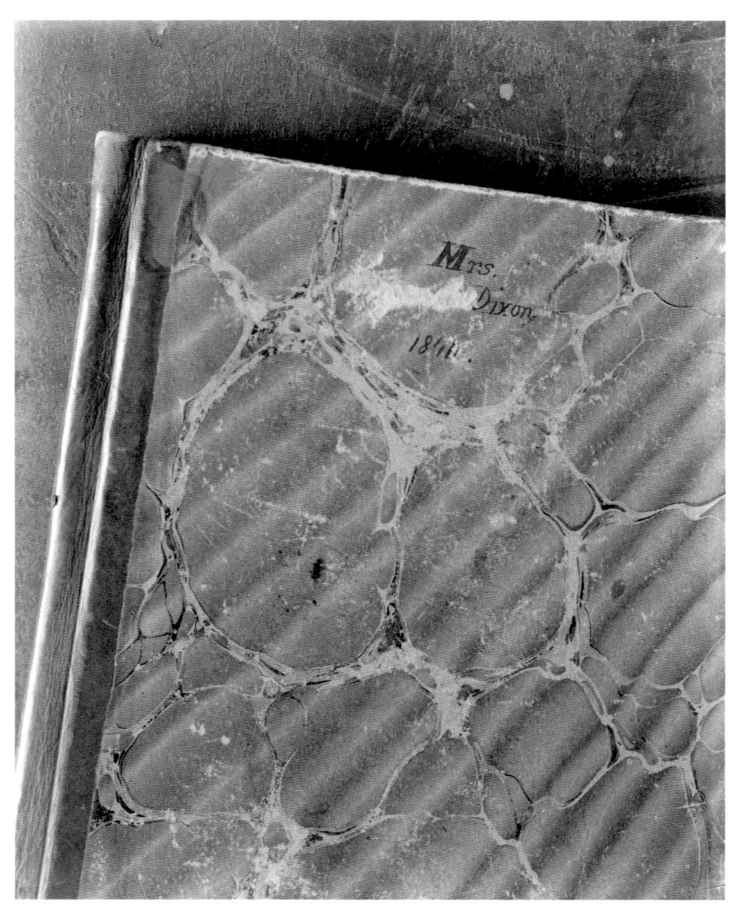
Mrs.
Dixon.
1841.

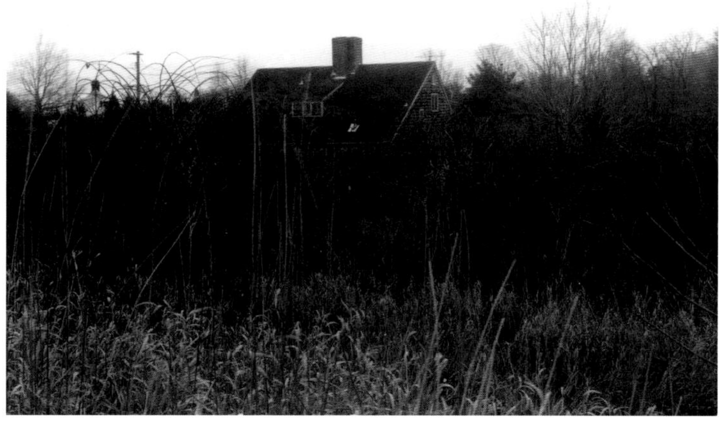

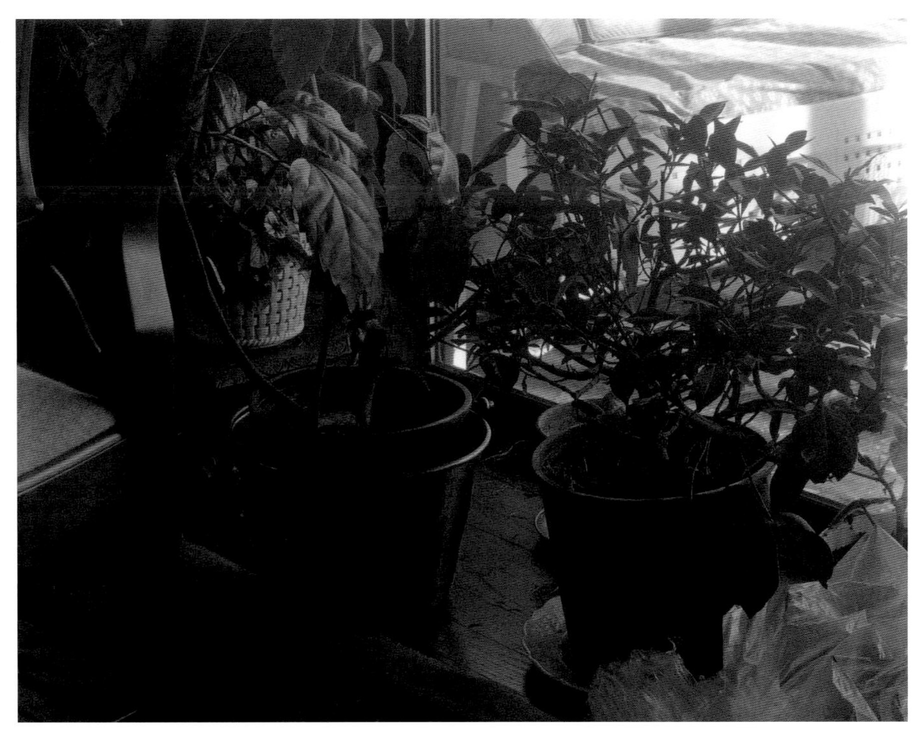

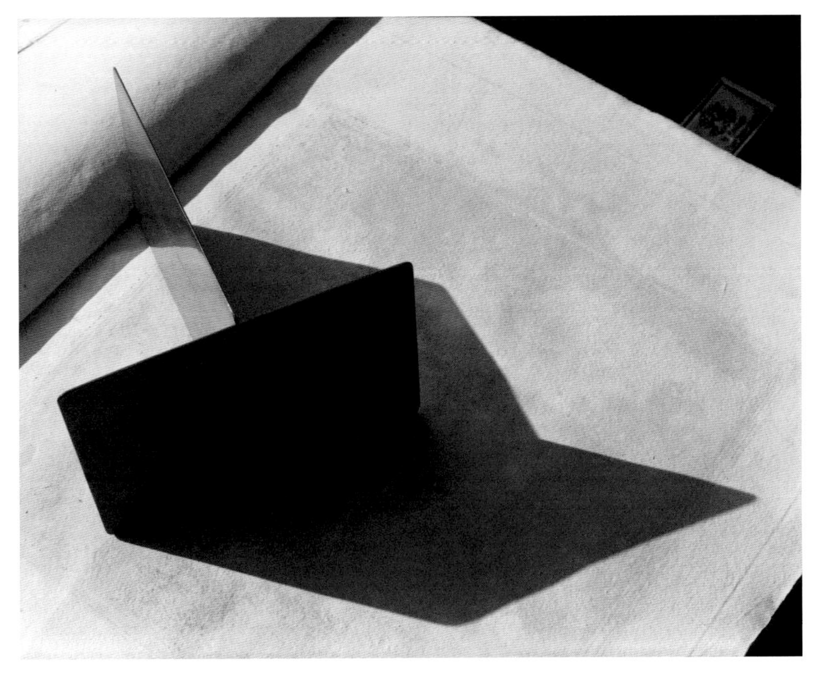

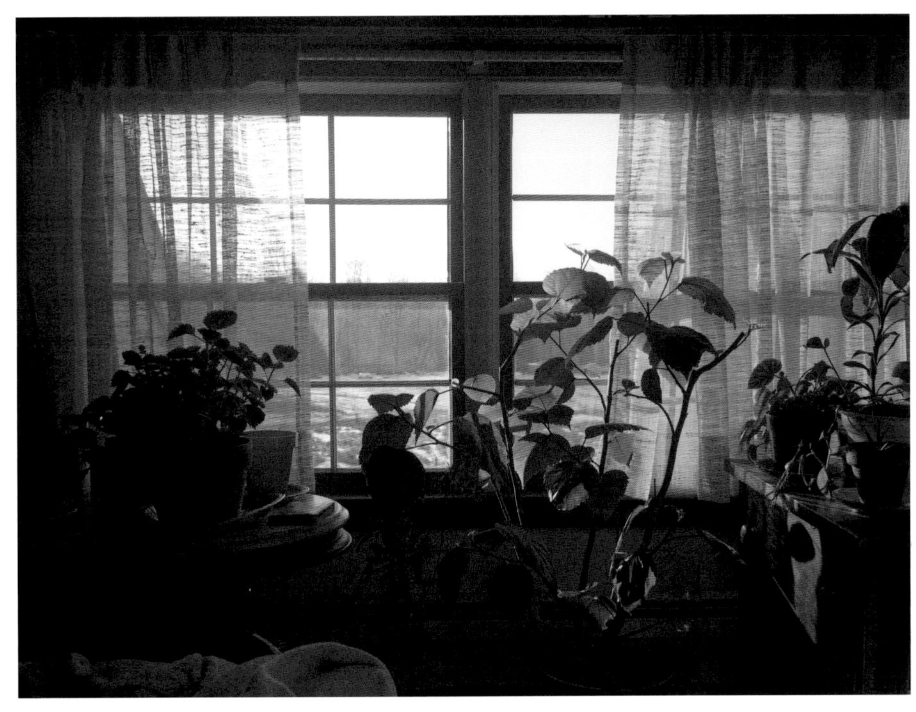

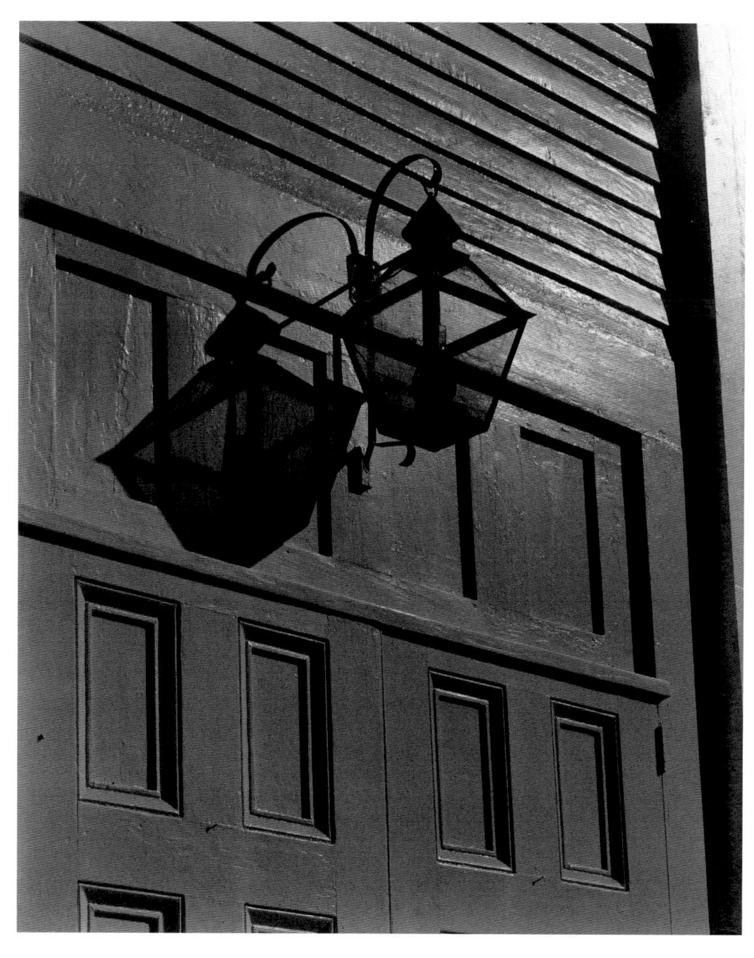

Sent & newspapers
Messrs Clarks who
Mr Imlay called in
nicely before dinner
Tuesday 17. In the
we went to see Mrs Sey
about leaving for ma
Mr Brimmer Mr Fre
Iglve who I told had
returned we called at
Boston who was "sorte
had a bad cold — then
Miss Gardiner but co
the evening there. a
had left one went for
then so we all went
at the piano. After
came in the smill
hat & came & Miss

early ... had se... two
...allie de français the
... a tailleur then Dr.
breakfast and then I
found her much wor...
for. but a few days;
her into spending the
of one thing and ano...
in my new white m...
crimson & lilac rose
lace tucker — black
trimmed with a clust...
a geranium of bri...
embroidered in

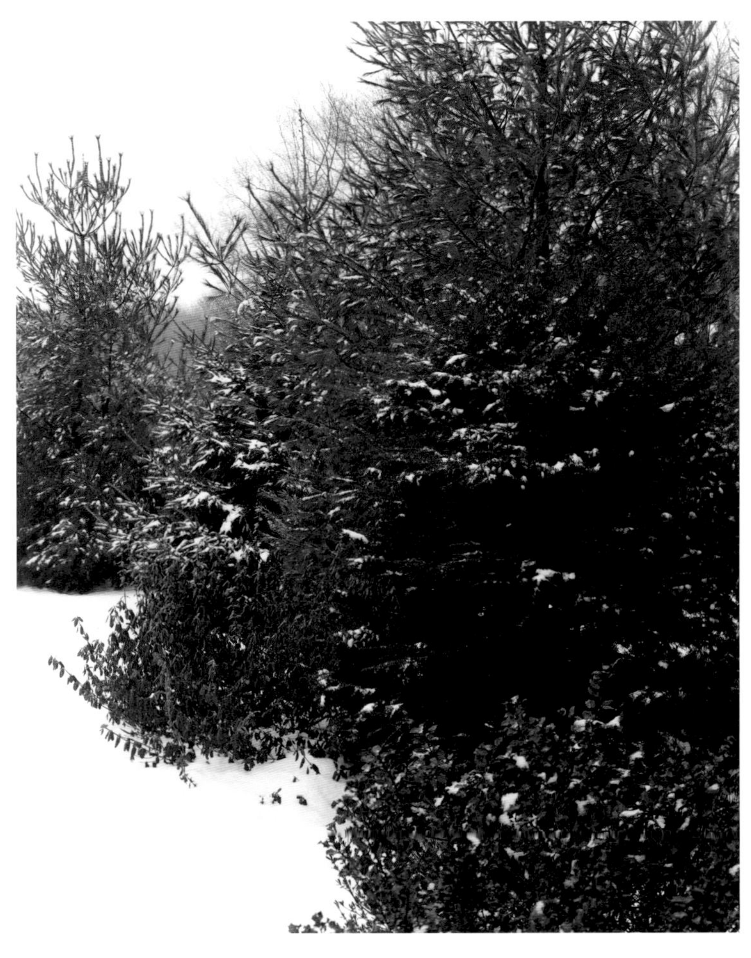

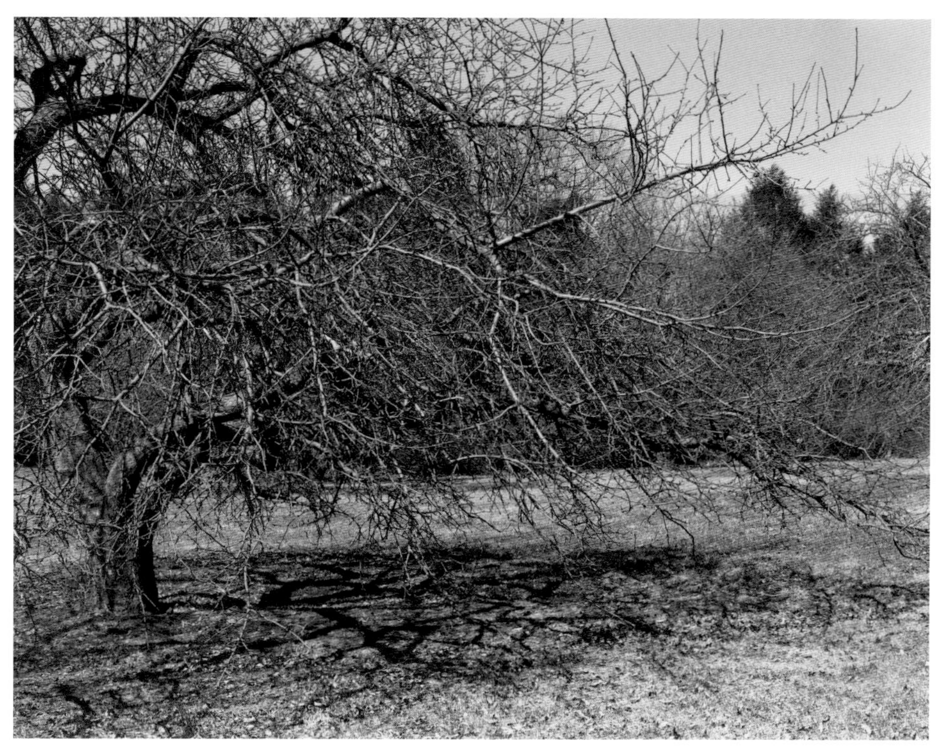

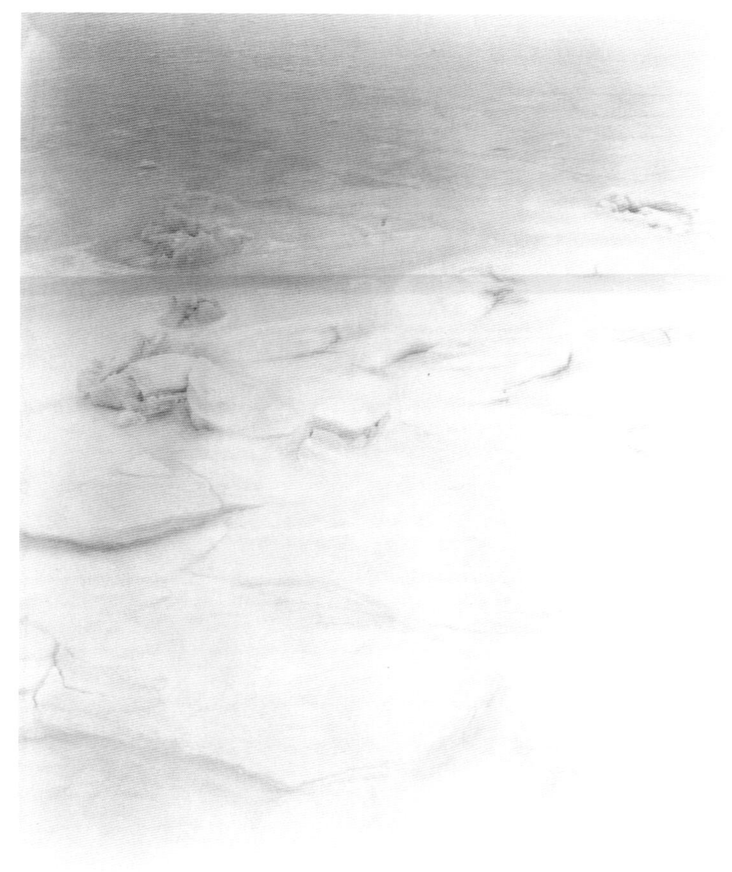

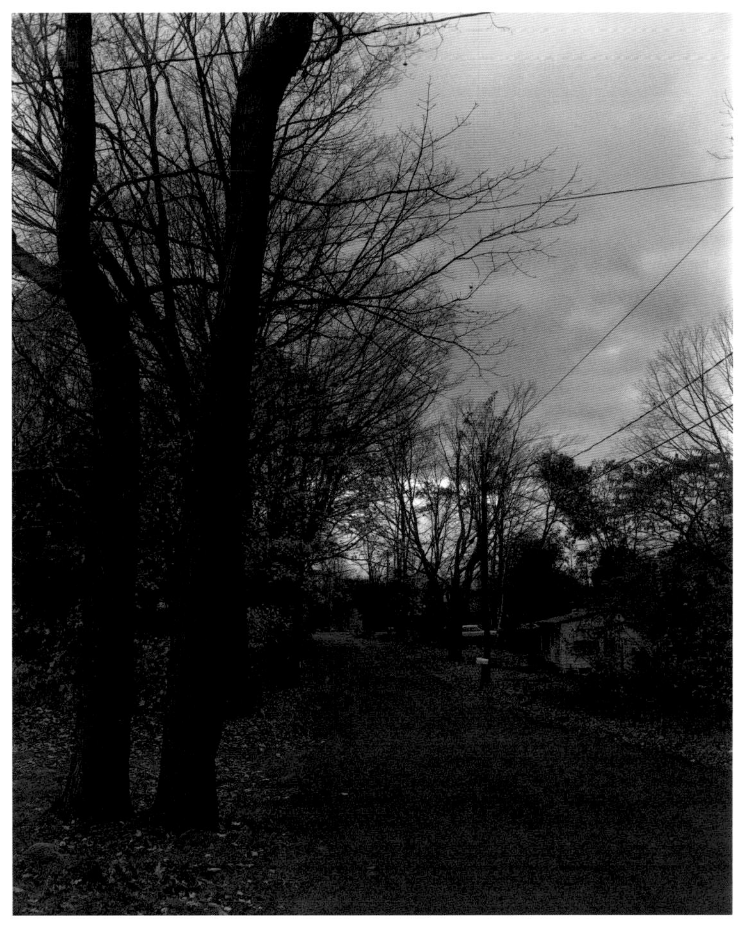

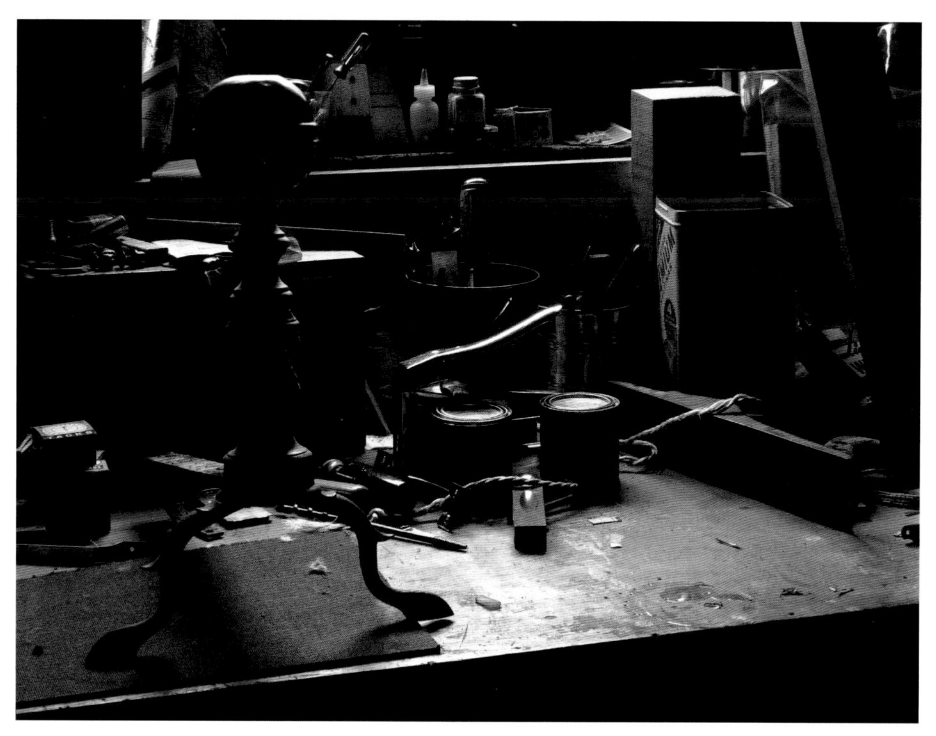

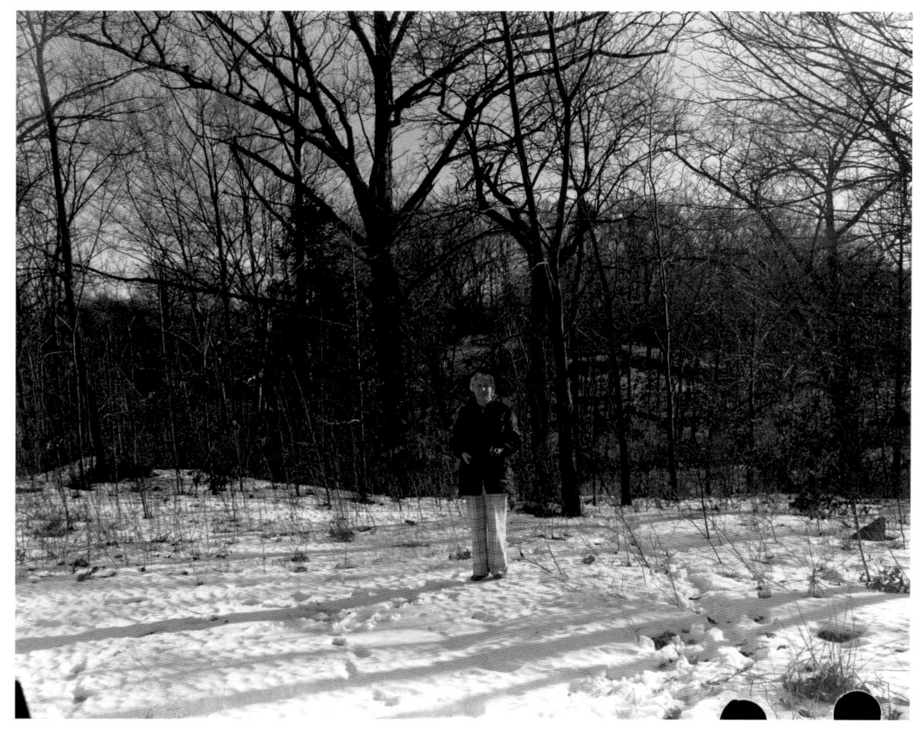

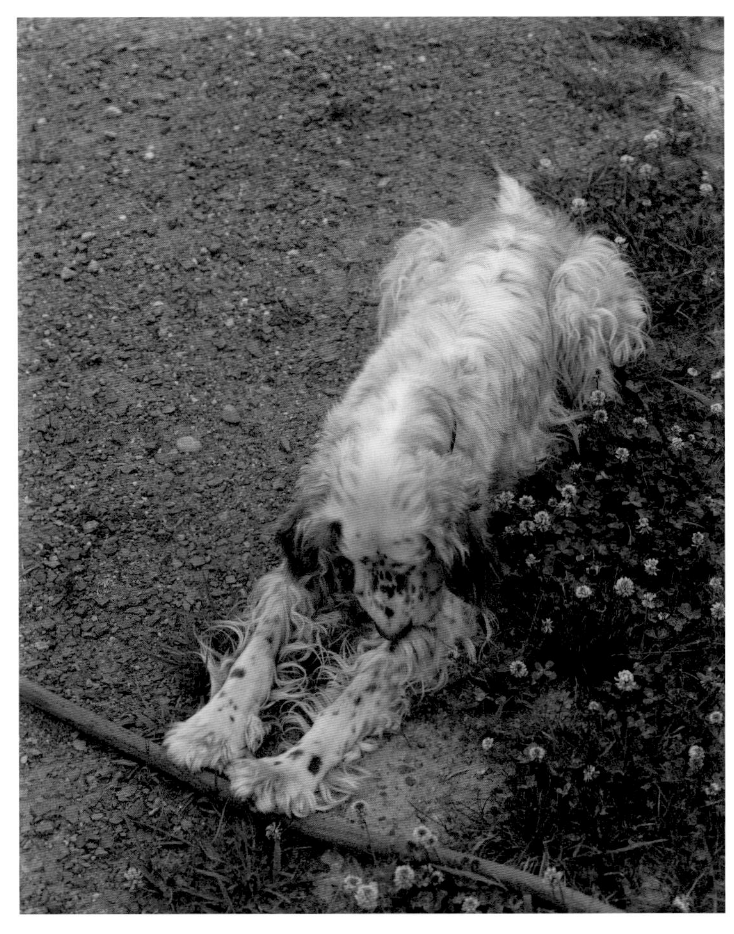

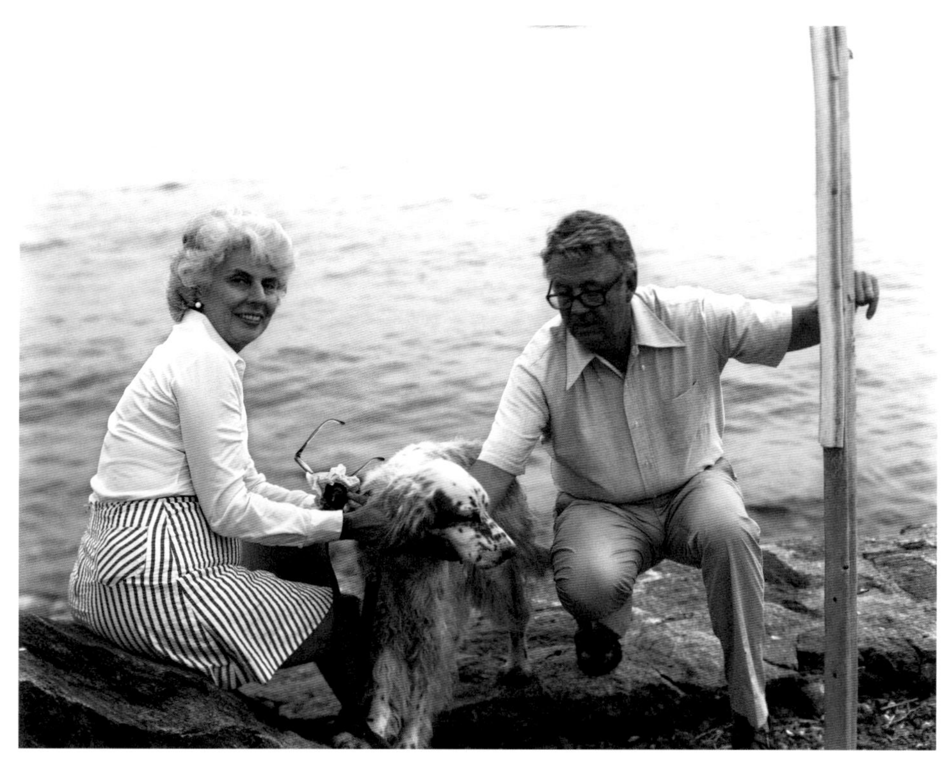

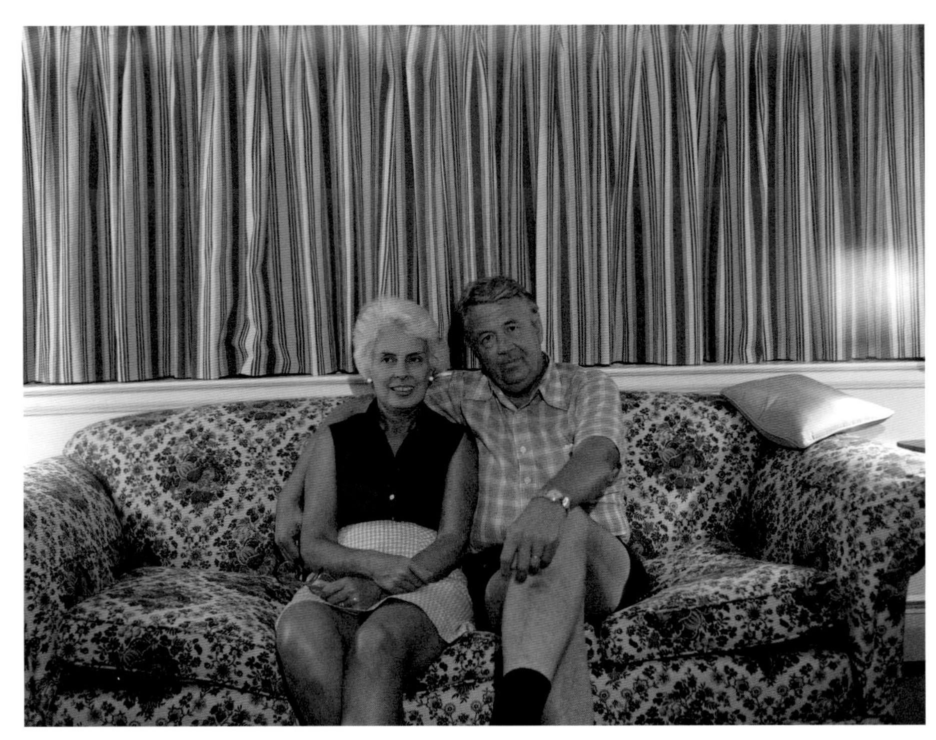

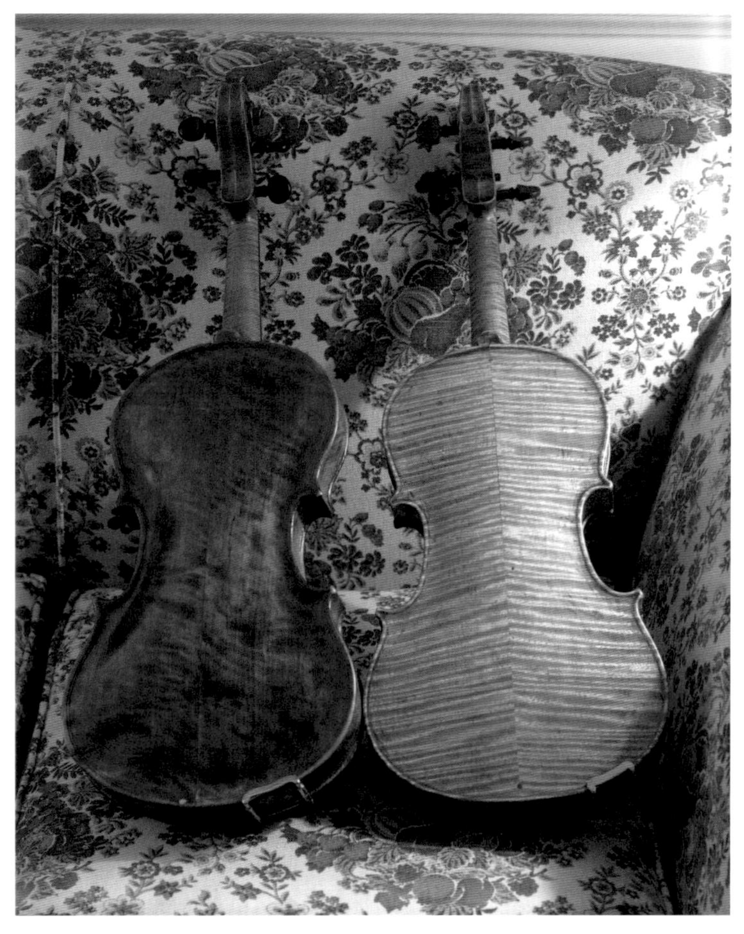

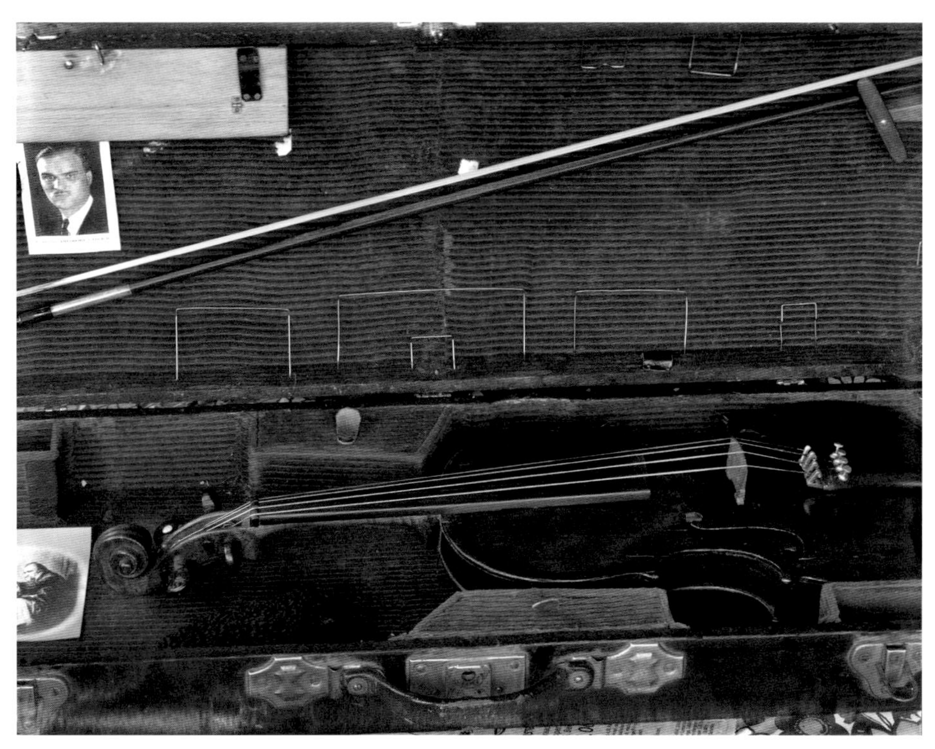

When I started photographing the diary in July 1977, I used a variety of 4 × 5 inch Kodak films: Plus X, Super XX, Royal Pan, Tri-X, and Ektapan. In 1978 I switched to Tri-X exclusively.

Almost all the Diary/Landscape images are on Azo, a slow-speed photographic paper manufactured by Kodak for making contact prints. A contact print is a very direct form of photographic printing: a sheet of Azo was placed in contact with a negative, exposed using an ordinary light bulb, and processed. The advantage of a slow-speed paper was that an absolutely light-proof room was not necessary. This was perfect for the ad hoc darkrooms I set up in the late 1970s. Furthermore, Azo had a tonal generosity that allowed me to make beautiful prints from my technically erratic negatives. I developed the prints in Kodak Dektol developer.

Early on I experimented with Kodak Studio Proof, a very slow printing-out paper that was also exposed by contact, in bright sunlight. The image appeared without developer, and when fully visible, it was washed in water, fixed, and toned (plates 7, 96, 13, 195, 42).

Negatives 1–106 were made in the summer of 1977, 107–129 in February 1978. Numbers 130–231 were made in 1979 and 232–295 in 1980. A few negatives after 295 date from 1981 to 1986.

JAMES WELLING

James Dixon was born in Enfield, Connecticut, in 1814. He studied law at Williams College and was admitted to the bar in 1834. In 1837 he was elected to the Connecticut State House of Representatives as a Whig. Elizabeth Lord Cogswell Dixon was born in Saco, Maine, in 1819 and attended Mrs. E. Smith's School in New York City. James and Elizabeth were married in 1840, at East Windsor Hill, Connecticut. The Dixons spent two years in Europe and kept a joint diary during their trip. Upon their return to Connecticut they settled in Asylum Hill in Hartford and raised four children. Following James's election to the US House of Representatives in 1845, the Dixons divided their time between Washington and Hartford. Elizabeth kept a detailed journal of their first two years in Washington (MS 67582 Connecticut Historical Society). In Hartford she was a friend of poet Lydia Sigourney, and later in Washington she was close to Mary Todd Lincoln, wife of the president. In 1857 James Dixon was elected to the US Senate as a Republican, where he served until 1869. Elizabeth died in 1871 and James in 1873.

ACKNOWLEDGMENTS

For over forty years I've traveled to my parents' home in Connecticut to make photographs. I started this pattern in earnest with *Diary/Landscape* in 1977, and I owe them my deepest thanks for all their love and encouragement.

In 1983 I met Frances Ferguson and Walter Benn Michaels, and their enthusiasm for my work was crucial in expanding my understanding of *Diary/Landscape* as it progressed.

My sincere thanks to Jack Goldstein, Saul Ostrow, Helene Winer, Janelle Reiring, Philip Nelson, Jay Gorney, Ronald Jones, Ann Goldstein, Ulrich Looch, Donald Young, Kiyoshi Wako, Leslie Tonkonow, Sarah Rogers, Helen Molesworth, Xavier Hufkens, Janice Guy, Loretta Yarlow, Anthony Spira, James Crump, Cindy Burlingham, Nigel Prince, and Thomas Seelig for exhibiting *Diary/Landscape*.

To Donald Young, who encouraged Matthew Witkovsky and the Art Institute of Chicago to acquire the complete *Diary/Landscape*, my profound thanks.

To Alan Thomas and Jill Shimabukuro at the University of Chicago Press, many thanks for the Press's sensitive articulation of *Diary/Landscape* as a book. My thanks as well to Danny Frank and his colleagues at Meridian Printing.

I am grateful to Regen Projects, Los Angeles; David Zwirner, New York/London; Maureen Paley, London; Peter Freeman, Inc., Paris; and the Comer Family Foundation for supporting this publication.

I want to thank my sister, Caroline Welling Van Deusen, who transcribed and published Elizabeth Dixon's Washington journal of 1845–47, for sharing with me her insights into the Dixons' personal lives.

Matthew Witkovsky, chair of the Department of Photography at the Art Institute of Chicago, made an initial suggestion that has been realized now with much care in this book and a concurrent exhibition at the Art Institute. I cannot imagine a more sensitive or insightful viewer of *Diary/Landscape*.

Finally, the University of Chicago Press joins me in thanking the Art Institute of Chicago for its collaboration on this project.

J. W.

ABOUT THE ARTIST
AND THE AUTHOR

JAMES WELLING was born in Hartford, Connecticut, in 1951, and studied art at Carnegie Mellon University and the California Institute of the Arts, where he received his MFA in 1974. His work has been the subject of survey exhibitions at the Kunsthalle Bern; Wexner Center for the Arts, Columbus; the Museum of Contemporary Art, Los Angeles; the Fotomuseum Winterthur, the Hammer Museum, Los Angeles; and the Cincinnati Art Museum. His books include *James Welling / The Mind on Fire*, *James Welling: Monograph*, *Glass House*, and *Light Sources*. In 2014 he received the International Center for Photography's Infinity Award in Art and he received the 1999 DG Bank-Förderpreis Fotografie from the Sprengel Museum in Hannover. He is a professor in the Department of Art at University of California, Los Angeles.

MATTHEW S. WITKOVSKY is Sandor Chair and curator of the Department of Photography at the Art Institute of Chicago. He studied art history at Yale University and the University of Pennsylvania, where he received his PhD in 2002. He is the author of *Light Years: Conceptual Art and the Photograph* and *Lewis Baltz: The Prototype Works*, with further essays in *Etudes Photographiques*, *Art Bulletin*, *October*, and other journals, as well as numerous exhibition catalogs. He is the recipient of the Kraszna-Krausz Book Award, the Vienna Art Book Award, and the Jan Masaryk Medal of the Ministry of Foreign Affairs of the Czech Republic.